THINKING CREATIVELY

❖ ❖ ❖ ❖ ❖ ❖ ❖ ❖ ❖ ❖ ❖

A New Approach to Psychology and Individual Lives

Leona E. Tyler

❖ ❖ ❖ ❖ ❖ ❖ ❖ ❖ ❖ ❖ ❖ ❖ ❖

THINKING CREATIVELY

Jossey-Bass Publishers
San Francisco • Washington • London • 1983

THINKING CREATIVELY
A New Approach to Psychology and Individual Lives
by Leona E. Tyler

Copyright © 1983 by: Jossey-Bass Inc., Publishers
433 California Street
San Francisco, California 94104
&
Jossey-Bass Limited
28 Banner Street
London EC1Y 8QE

Library of Congress Cataloging in Publication Data

Tyler, Leona Elizabeth (date)
Thinking creatively.

Bibliography: p. 203
Includes index.
1. Creative thinking. I. Title.
BF408.T94   1983   150'.1   83-48166
ISBN 0-87589-585-9

Manufactured in the United States of America

The paper in this book meets the guidelines for
permanence and durability of the Committee on
Production Guidelines for Book Longevity of the
Council on Library Resources.

JACKET DESIGN BY WILLI BAUM

FIRST EDITION

Code 8332

The Jossey-Bass
Social and Behavioral Science Series

PREFACE

On a fine spring day in Amsterdam in 1963, as I tried to make sense of some research results stemming from a stimulating sabbatical year, a thought came to me that was to set the direction for all my thinking from that time to the present. It was the idea that for every situation in which human beings are involved there is more than one *possible* outcome. Only one, of course, is actualized, and after its occurrence this one appears to have been inevitable.

I explored the implications of this assumption first in the realm with which I was most familiar, that of individual differences and human development. The results of this undertaking have been brought together in my 1978 book, *Individuality: Human Possibilities and Personal Choice in the Psychological Development of Men and Women*. In the present book I extend the search for implications to other areas. In both these books I hope to communicate with the increasing number of producers and users of psychological knowledge who have become dissatisfied with the directions in which our science has been moving and who find the oft-stated objective of the whole effort "to predict and control behavior" an unappealing and probably unattainable goal. The intended audience includes thoughtful students, experienced researchers and clinicians, and specialists

in the social sciences and humanities who are concerned about
the impact of psychology on their disciplines. Note that a psychologist who has specialized in one of the areas covered in the
chapters on perception, learning, and other topics will likely
find the overview of trends in his or her field elementary or
oversimplified. I have deliberately pruned away much of the
foliage in order to reveal the main outlines of trunk and
branches. The chapters are not written for specialists in the particular areas but for psychologists in other areas, such as learning researchers who wish to understand what has been going on
in social psychology, clinicians who wish to know more about
cognitive science, and generalists seeking an overview of the
whole psychological enterprise.

For a time I attempted to put together a structure of possibility theory complete with axioms, corollaries, and testable
hypotheses, but somehow such a structure did not work. The
concept of multiple possibilities is not really a foundation stone
that supports a structure but rather a stone dropped into the
flowing river of psychological thinking, ripples from which
spread out in all directions. This is the metaphor that underlies
the book. It discusses what the implications would be of adopting a basic assumption that any situation has more than one
possible outcome, only one of which can be actualized, and
that the particular outcome is not *completely* determined by
causal factors preceding it.

Three aspects of the basic idea became apparent to me as
I proceeded. The first is that in the underlying nature of things,
one *need not assume complete determinism*; there is always
some "play" in the system. The second aspect is an emphasis
on *multiplicity*. Before an event occurs, it is one among several
possible events, many of which we may not see unless we search
for them. The third aspect is an emphasis on conscious *choice*
as a way of transforming plural possibilities into a singular actuality. One or another of these three ideas is brought in again
and again in the discussions of psychological research and practice.

In the two introductory chapters that constitute Part
One, I relate the central idea to important ideas that have re-

cently appeared in the biological and physical sciences and in the philosophy of science in general and psychological science in particular. I make use of Popper's concept of *World 3,* using it to include not only the totality of scientific knowledge mankind has generated but also folklore, mythology, and literature —in short, the whole symbolic environment. Cultures and individuals adapt to it by *selecting* from the multitude of possibilities it provides, a process analogous to the selection of ecological niches by different plants and animals in the course of biological evolution. Organized selections from World 3 can thus be thought of as symbolic *habitats* in which human beings live and to which they adapt. Conscious choice can play a large part in the selection of habitat. General systems theory is presented as a basis for research techniques more appropriate for this orientation than the causal models used most frequently in the past.

In the five chapters of Part Two I discuss what this approach means for research on perception, learning and memory, cognitive science, social psychology, and developmental psychology. Ways in which multiple possibilities have become apparent even when researchers were not looking for them are pointed out, and the importance of devoting more attention to them in theorizing, designing experiments, analyzing data, and interpreting results is emphasized.

Part Three takes up the meaning of the concept of multiple possibilities for three major specializations within applied psychology: childrearing, therapy and counseling, and self-management. In each chapter the body of psychological knowledge and skills that has accumulated over the years is summarized in an organized way, and the value of the proposed orientation in utilizing it is shown. The importance of choice is again emphasized. In the final chapter the relationship of the concept of multiple possibilities to probability theory, on which so much of psychological thinking is based in both the research and the applied areas, is analyzed, and some of the most significant new ideas from previous chapters are highlighted.

To all its readers, the book brings an invitation to think creatively about the basic questions that concern us all. Whether or not readers agree with me about the significance of my basic concept is of little moment. What is important is that we all draw from the storehouse of our accumulated knowledge and experience the core ideas that have proved most meaningful to us and make them available as possibilities for others to use.

The writers who have influenced my thinking are far too numerous to mention in detail. Some of the most important are cited in the text and included in the reference list. Talking to students, clients, and colleagues, especially Robert Leeper and Norman Sundberg, has also been a stimulating experience. I express my appreciation to all these people, those I know personally and those I know only from what they have written. What I think of now as the original source of my theorizing was a seminar in which I participated as a graduate student many years ago—R. M. Elliott's course titled Human Behavior. Dr. Elliott no longer lives, but I still think of him with appreciation and affection as a major influence on my life as a psychologist.

Eugene, Oregon   Leona E. Tyler
September 1983

CONTENTS

THE AUTHOR

✤　✤　✤　✤　✤　✤　✤　✤　✤　✤　✤　✤

Leona Elizabeth Tyler, who served as dean of the graduate school at the University of Oregon from 1965 until her retirement in 1971, began her long association with the university in 1940.

Her degrees were earned at the University of Minnesota: a B.S. in English in 1925, a M.S. in psychometrics in 1939, and a Ph.D. in psychology in 1941. After receiving her bachelor's degree, she taught for thirteen years in junior high schools in Minnesota and Michigan. In the course of this experience, she came to appreciate the unique qualities of individuals, especially as revealed in her students' compositions.

Leona Tyler has served as president of the Oregon Psychological Association (1953-1954), the Western Psychological Association (1957-1958), and the American Psychological Association (1972-1973). She has held guest professorships at the University of California, Berkeley (1957-1958), and the University of Amsterdam (1962-1963), with summer appointments at Stanford University, the University of British Columbia, and the University of Minnesota.

Her research undertakings have focused mainly on the development of interests and organized choices; counseling has also been one of her professional concerns throughout the years, and she has published a number of papers in these areas. She is the author of *Tests and Measurements* (1979, 3rd ed., with W. B. Walsh), *Individuality: Human Possibilities and Personal Choice in the Psychological Development of Men and Women* (1978), *Individual Differences: Abilities and Motivational Directions* (1974), *The Work of the Counselor* (1969, 3rd ed.), and *The Psychology of Human Differences* (1965, 3rd ed.). She is the editor of *Intelligence: Some Recurring Issues* (1969) and a collaborator with N. Sundberg and J. Taplin on *An Introduction to Clinical Psychology* (1983) and *Clinical Psychology: Expanding Horizons* (1973), with N. Sundberg on *Clinical Psychology: An Introduction to Research and Practice* (1962), and with F. Goodenough on a revision of *Developmental Psychology* (1959).

Leona Tyler now divides her time between her home at Heceta Beach on the Oregon coast and an apartment in Eugene. Since retirement, she has traveled extensively in Europe, Asia, and the South Pacific.

PART I

Thinking Creatively
About Multiple Possibilities

❖ ❖ ❖ ❖ ❖ ❖ ❖ ❖ ❖ ❖ ❖ ❖

CHAPTER 1

Psychology as a Science of Life

❖ ❖ ❖ ❖ ❖ ❖ ❖ ❖ ❖ ❖ ❖ ❖

The concept of multiple possibilities has never occupied a very important place in psychology. The psychologist's ideal world has been a fixed one governed by uniform causal laws, one in which all events are in principle explainable and predictable. It is true that psychologists seldom, if ever, encounter such uniform causal sequences in the individuals they study, but they attribute this fact to the complexity of the phenomena being observed. We like to assume that "what is" is completely determined by "what was" and that the roots of "what is to be" are already growing and discoverable.

According to psychology's conventional wisdom, the goal of science is to "predict and control" the phenomena it studies, and therefore the aim of psychology must be to predict and control behavior. It has been our faith that as research techniques improved, we would be able to make more and more accurate predictions and exercise more and more complete control over recalcitrant human nature. But as decade succeeds decade, we somehow never seem to get any closer to this goal. The best we can do is to make moderately accurate statistical predictions about general trends in groups of people. What *individuals* do continues to surprise us. Why is this? Could it be that at any instant in time there are several possible futures, each of which is linked as closely as the others to the circumstances preceding it? It is this basic hypothesis that I will examine in detail.

While psychologists have been ignoring the problem of conceptualizing possibilities, philosophers century after century have struggled with it. In modern times the most influential figure was Leibniz, who proposed the concept of "possible worlds": God could have created any one of an infinite number of worlds, in each of which objects and their relationships might have been very different from what they are in the world we know. But because God chose this one, "the best of all possible worlds," everything it contains and everything that happens within it must be as they are. A recent book (Loux, 1979) offers a number of contemporary views. The most promising one (Rescher, 1975) breaks with the Leibnizian tradition, presenting the thesis that the basic distinction between the actual and the possible is that possibilities are not primary realities but are intellectual constructions made from materials in the realm of the actual. Instead of possibility being prior to actuality, as Leibniz would have it, it is derived from and built on actuality. This idea would seem to be of special interest to psychologists, in that it makes possibility a psychological, rather than a theological or metaphysical, concept. We can begin with the assumption that thinking beings *create* possibilities—and that these newly created bits of the universe take their places in the complex of factors determining the future.

Some Basic Biological Ideas

Ever since psychology set out to become a science, it has not been much influenced by what philosophers were saying. The models for the discipline have been mainly physics and chemistry. In our time, however, more and more voices are being raised to suggest that biology is a more appropriate model, as human beings are first of all living creatures. And many biologists now believe that the biological sciences differ from the physical sciences in many aspects of their structure. The difference is not simply one of complexity. The assumption that all living processes can be reduced to physical and chemical laws has become increasingly untenable as knowledge has accumulated. This shift in thinking does not mean that vitalism has reappeared or that any nonnatural principle must be postulated. What biological scientists are saying is that "the strategy of research in biology must . . . be quite different from the strategy of the physicist" (Mayr, 1976, p. 14). At the same time, advanced thinking in physics and chemistry is bringing those fields closer in some ways to biology than to the nineteenth-century theories that have dominated psychology (Prigogine, 1980). I shall touch on these ideas later. But first let us look at some of the biological "givens" on which strategy should be based.

Probably the most basic fact is the staggering *diversity* of the living world. In the first place, the number of species is astronomically large. Over the centuries biologists have repeatedly changed their definition of what constitutes a species, and there is still no unanimity about the definition. Typological definitions based on morphological similarities prevailed for a long view, but they have proved inadequate. Definitions based on interbreeding are more satisfactory. Whether or not individuals of the same species look alike, they do share a common gene pool, different from that of other species. What distinguishes species living in the same locality is the fact that they do not interbreed. Mayr (1976, p. 519), defining species in this way, says the following about their number:

> Few nontaxonomists have any conception of the magnitude of biological diversity. More than a million species of animals have already been described and nearly half a million species of plants. However, our knowledge is highly uneven. Only about three new species of birds are described annually, a very small addition to the 8,600 species

previously recorded. But let us look at some other groups. I still remember the days when many papers were published in the genetic literature giving the name of the organism simply as *Drosophila*. This was implicitly considered to be synonymous with *D. melanogaster*. Now more than 1,000 species of *Drosophila* are recognized and almost as many new species were discovered in the last seventeen years as in the 170 years preceding 1950. . . . What the total of species of animals is, no one knows. It may be three million, it may be five million, and it may even be ten million.

But the extent of the diversity among living creatures goes far beyond the diversity of species. Every individual member of each of these millions of species, at least those that reproduce sexually, is unique. Each begins life with a different set of genetic determiners. Diversity and uniqueness—these are the characteristics that distinguish the subject matter of biology from that of physics and chemistry and demand from the scientist a different research strategy and a different approach to theory.

If diversity and uniqueness are characteristic of living matter generally, they are more characteristic of human beings and the higher animals. Consider, for example, the number of pairings that may occur when random halves of the gene pairs in each of the twenty-three chromosomes combine with random halves of those from the other twenty-three. The number is almost inconceivably large, even if we ignore the effects of mutations and other genetic irregularities. With the exception of identical twins, no two individuals are alike when life begins, and no two, not even twins, encounter exactly the same influences as they grow.

Within the individual, cells themselves are diverse and unique. Young (1978, p. 44) calls attention to this complexity. "There are said to be about ten thousand million nerve cells in the human cortex (10^{10}). . . . But the really important fact is that no two of them are exactly alike." It is this tremendous diversity that makes it possible for combinations of cells to record changes occurring in the outside world, to store memory records, and to initiate actions. And it is this diversity that makes the glibly stated "predict and control" objective forever unattainable. There are just too many ways that psychological events can take place.

Multiple possibilities arise from the mathematical fact that a limited number of units can be *combined* in so many ways. And when numbers become so large, the amount of *time* it would take to inventory them, even with the aid of a high-speed computer, makes complete analysis impossible. Whatever one believes about determinism as an underlying characteristic of the universe, one must resign oneself to dealing with different effects following on what appears to be the same cause and with different causes producing what appears to be the same effect. Multiple possibility is a fact of life.

The attempt to impose predictability on the multifarious living world has a long history. The most persistent and durable of the metaphysical systems growing out of this attempt is the complex of ideas that make up the ontological theory of "the great chain of being" (Lovejoy, 1936). Going back to Plato's *Timaeus,* and promulgated by Aristotle, it rested on three major propositions. The first was that, because of the infinite creativity of God, all things possible actually exist. Or, to put it the opposite way, there is nothing possible that does not actually exist. The second proposition was that being is *continuous,* with no gaps between parts. Nature does not make leaps. All classifications, including those we use in distinguishing living species, are only tools we find necessary to use in our thinking, limited as human intelligence is; lower species shade gradually into higher ones. The third proposition was that the whole chain of being constitutes a *quantitative* scale extending from the simplest organisms to the most complex. The human race does not necessarily occupy the uppermost rung of this enormous ladder. Medieval theologians took it for granted that there were orders of heavenly beings as superior to us as we are to earthworms.

Lovejoy shows how, as centuries passed, this scheme was assimilated to successive patterns of philosophical thinking, though not without allowance being made for conflicts and inconsistencies. Each generation of philosophers found ways of reconciling these difficulties for its own age. During the seventeenth and eighteenth centuries, the whole system was given a time dimension. Creation was not assumed to have been instantaneous, but the basic outlines were preserved. It was believed that over the centuries God's creative power was bringing all possible things into existence and that the trend was toward higher and higher levels of perfection. Evolutionists before Darwin found this way of thinking congenial, and many people in our time continue to hold somewhat similar views. The appeal of such views is that they make for optimism about the future, although it has always been difficult to reconcile some aspects of the present with the assumption of God's infinite goodness.

According to Mayr (1976, p. 290), the essence of the Darwinian revolution was that "instead of endorsing the eighteenth-century concept of a drive toward perfection, Darwin merely postulated change." It was this idea, rather than the theory of evolution itself, which called for a radical reconceptualization of the world system and which led to the prolonged controversies following publication of *On the Origin of Species* in 1859. As Mayr puts it, "Darwin's conclusion was that evolutionary change through adaptation and specialization by no means necessitates continuous betterment. This view proved very unpopular and is even today largely ignored by nonbiologists. . . . The main reason evolutionism, particularly in its Darwinian form, made slow progress is that it was the replacement of one entire *Weltanschauung* by a different one. This involved religion, philosophy, and humanism" (pp. 292-293).

Although psychologists generally pride themselves on having cut the Gordian knot of philosophical speculation, one can still find traces in current thinking of assumptions inherent in pre-Darwinian thinking about the "great chain of being." Psychologists do not argue that because of God's infinite creativeness all possibilities exist, but they do ignore the nonactualized possibilities implicit in every situation and assume that what happens is in principle predictable. And thus their stance is a perpetuation of the old metaphysics. Similarly, the assumption that everything can be scaled and all differences expressed as amount or degree is basically a pre-Darwinian idea, resting on the belief that differences between species and between individuals can be ordered along a single dimension. Psychologists, it is true, are not interested in a long linear scale ranging from amebas to humans (or angels). But they do assume that, for any segment of the scale, the phenomena in which they are interested can be *measured,* not simply described or categorized. The act of measurement imposes on the phenomena a less/more or lower/higher structure. Research that simply states what subjects did or classifies their responses into different categories is considered less elegant and less definitive than research obtaining quantitative results. Probably no sentence has been quoted more frequently by psychologists than Thorndike's dictum that everything that exists exists in quantity and can be measured.

This quantitative bias is not characteristic of modern evolutionary thinking. The differences among the several million identified species are seen to be basically qualitative, not quantitative. We have no justification for assuming that all differences between individuals or groups can be measured or that all differences between experimental and control groups can be expressed in numerical form. These have been simplifying assumptions that have enabled psychologists to get on with their research tasks, but as the full complexity of what we are investigating comes into view, other assumptions, other strategies, other research tools must be created. Mayr (1976, p. 317) highlights this idea: "The more I study evolution the more I am impressed by the uniqueness, by the unpredictability of evolutionary events. Let me end this discussion with the provocative question: 'Is it not perhaps a basic error of methodology to apply such a generalizing technique as mathematics to a field of unique events, such as organic evolution?' "

This book is a search for other ways of conceptualizing psychological reality and other ways of studying it.

Habitats and Evolution

Darwin's great contribution was to demonstrate that the diversity of living creatures could be accounted for by natural selection, although the demonstration was never completely convincing. Recently there has been a resurgence of interest in exploring other factors underlying *macroevolution*—meaning the occurrence of new species. The world we inhabit consists of an almost infinite variety of *habitats*—hot desert sands, polar icecaps, coral reefs, caverns deep in the ocean, tropical forests, grasslands, rural villages, crowded cities—the list could be continued indefinitely. During the millions of years that life has existed on earth, living creatures repeatedly ventured into new environmental niches. Individuals that could not adapt to the new conditions perished, but because of genetic diversity within each species, some had the genetic makeup to survive to reproductive age, thus ensuring that genes facilitating adaptation were more plentiful than they were in the original migrants. Thus new species arose, according to Darwin, as over the generations the gene pool changed enough to preclude interbreeding. Whether or not this basic idea is modified or supplemented by further research, it has served science well as an organizing principle in biology and many other fields, psychology among them.

To explain natural selection in this way is, of course, a simplification. Gene pools constantly change through mutation. Environments also undergo constant change. Organisms can have different ways of adapting to the same habitat, and habitats providing *Lebensraum* for many very different species can coexist in the same geographical space. Over a thousand million years, some portions of the earth's surface have become colder or warmer, drier or wetter, completely submerged under water or totally dry. Countless species have come into existence, and countless have become extinct. But natural selection continues to operate and adaptation continues to occur. Every area of the earth's surface provides a wide variety of specialized habitats. Along the rocky shores of the Pacific, sea urchins and crabs, sandpipers and seagulls, flounders and octopuses all flourish, each making use of just that combination of rock and sand, water and sunlight, plant and animal matter carried by the currents that it needs to maintain life. Each species finds its own *ecological niche,* and each constitutes a part of the habitat of the others.

For some species, such as migrating birds and whales,

habitats are very large, extending from arctic to tropical zones. Some species of birds are at home in Asia, Europe, and America, wherever the general environmental features on which they depend are present. For species of this sort, different subspecies, or "races," can often be identified. For example, the red cross-bill (*Loxia curvirostra*) originated in the mountains of central Asia. Spreading out toward the periphery of its range, this species gradually colonized a number of similar geographical areas as far away as northern Europe, the United States, and Central America. Some changes occurred as it adapted to regional differences. Races that fed on spruce or larch, including the original Asian variety, developed thin, slender bills. Those that moved to an area where pines predominate developed larger, heavier bills (Mayr, 1976, pp. 148-149). Natural selection produces these differences. In a pine-growing area, birds with tough bills can open pine cones and thus stand a better chance of surviving and breeding; genetic diversity within the species provides enough of these favored individuals so that the frequency of their genes in the population increases.

The concept of multiple possibilities becomes important here. The habitat of a species or subspecies can be thought of as a *selection* from the possibilities for adaptation that an environment provides. To quote Mayr again, "The adaptation for life in a given habitat includes the faculty of the individual of the species to select this habitat (from a vast array of possible ones!) during the dispersal phase" (p. 149). And a dispersal phase seems to occur in the life cycle of most species studied. During this phase, "many individuals are carried into unsuitable locations and perish. . . . An occasional individual may have an unusually favorable gene combination that will permit some of its descendants to flourish in the new locality" (p. 149). Habitats change constantly, and it is only the fact of genetic diversity that enables a species to survive.

The study of the habitats of the many species of living things in the same geographical area and of the interrelationships between them is a flourishing branch of biology, the science of *ecology*. Only since midcentury, however, has *ecological psychology* emerged as a specialty. It began when Roger Barker and his associates set up the Midwest Psychological Field Station in a little town in Kansas and undertook to record all the behavior of the 119 children in the community's various behavior settings. Since the first book resulting from this project, *One Boy's Day* (Barker and Wright, 1951), a steady stream of findings about the nature of psychological habitats has been published. A good overview is presented in Barker and Associates (1978). New data-gathering and data-processing techniques have been invented and repeatedly modified, new constructs and theories elaborated. This body of work constitutes a step toward a biological, rather than a physical, model for psychology. And now many psychologists besides those in the Kansas group specialize in ecological psychology (Stokols, 1978).

As mentioned earlier, not all present-day evolutionists find the Darwinian theory of natural selection completely satisfying: It does not quite explain everything. One problem taken up by the paleontologist Gould (1980) has some relevance to psychology. Gould thinks that in addition to the principle of selection through adaptation we need another principle. He emphasizes that although the number of variations on which the differentiation of species and subspecies rests is very large, it is not infinite. Some variations that would be adaptive do not in fact occur, and some variations that contribute nothing to adaptation persist for generations. Gould suggests that *structural integration* is a factor in evolution. Because living creatures are shaped by an embryological process that to some extent recapitulates earlier evolutionary stages, some kinds of structures can develop and others cannot. Only *variations in these structures* are available for natural selection to work on. "Evolution is, as Francois Jacob perceptively stated, a tinkerer, not a noble architect" (Gould, 1980, p. 45).

To follow Gould's ideas a bit further, each structural constraint carries with it possibilities for consequences completely unrelated to the adaptive function it originally served, and these possibilities can produce novel consequences at a later time. An outstanding example of structural integration is the human brain. Whatever the adaptive advantage it originally gave our early forebears over ape competitors, it has proved far more useful for the multitude of purposes it later came to serve. Gould says succinctly, "Original function does not determine potential use" (p. 47). His concept of constraints and consequences provides a useful building block for a theory of multiple possibilities. The potential uses for any evolved living structure are manifold.

Over the years evolutionary theorists have confronted a basic problem: Evolution seems to contradict one of the most basic laws of physics, the second law of thermodynamics. In the physical world, energy transformations progress from the more to the less complex, from order to disorder or randomness. This increasing disorder is what is meant by *entropy*. In evolution, the opposite trend is apparent, from less to more complex ordered arrangements. What is perhaps one of the most important new ideas of recent times explains away this paradox and carries evolutionary theory beyond the Darwinian formulation. Prigogine (1980) performed chemical experiments (for which he received a Nobel prize) showing that even in nonliving matter it is possible for increases rather than decreases in order and complexity to occur. In an open system, where energy exchanges with the environment take place, order may emerge because of entropy, not in spite of it. The reason is that such systems are constantly *fluctuating*. If the fluctuations reach a critical size so that equilibrium cannot be restored, a giant perturbation results in a sudden shift to a new kind of organization more complex than the former one, exporting or *dissipating* entropy into the environment; the total amount of entropy is the same but complexity has increased. Prigogine called these suddenly emerging dynamic organizations *dissipative structures*.

Evolutionary theorists are realizing the importance of this concept. Jantsch (1980) uses it as the foundation for a comprehensive theory dealing with the long sequence of transformations that have occurred in our universe, from energy to matter, to large molecules, to single cells without nuclei (prokaryotes), to complexly organized single cells (eukaryotes), to higher forms of plants and animals, to human beings, to ecosystems and societies. Basic to the whole theory is the idea that dissipative structures are not formed in the same way and do not obey the same laws as the equilibrium structures with which we are more familiar. Three conditions are necessary for *order through fluctuation*: (1) openness of the system to the environment, (2) high *non*equilibrium, and (3) internal reinforcement of fluctuations. Jantsch's discussion, some of it highly speculative, contends that these conditions were present at each stage where an evolutionary transformation occurred. This new way of looking at the material world does much more than explain how evolution is possible. It stimulates psychologists, brain scientists, sociologists, artists, and philosophers to reexamine their theories about change. It suggests that we expect and make use of unpredicted changes, novel structures and organizations, unprecedented developments. Creativity is liberated. I began this chapter suggesting that psychology model itself on biology rather than physics. It now seems that both psychologists and physical scientists must learn to think about processes and systems in a manner that is closer to biology than to the standard physics and chemistry of the past.

The Theory of Living Systems

The advance in theoretical thinking could not have occurred had there not already been taking place an active movement to replace mechanistic theories by *general systems theory*. This theory recognizes that the most salient fact about living creatures (and many aggregations of people and things) is that every part is related to every other part, so that a change anywhere produces a change everywhere. Miller (1978), building on the ideas of Bertalanffy (1968) and others, has produced the most complete version of the theory. To begin with, he points out nine characteristics found in all living systems:

1. Living systems are *open* rather than closed and have inputs, throughputs, and outputs that process matter and energy, on the one hand, and information, on the other.
2. For a time such a system *counteracts entropy*, the universal tendency of matter to move toward a dispersed, inert state. (Prigogine's work, discussed earlier, though not available to Miller at the time he was writing, is relevant here.)

3. Systems show *complexity,* or differentiation of parts.
4. They contain basic *blueprints* that control their functioning—DNA for individuals, charters or bylaws for large groups.
5. They are made up of *macromolecules* and may include nonliving components.
6. They contain *subsystems,* the most critical of which is the *decider.*
7. They carry on processes through their own subsystems but may make use of nonliving material outside their boundaries.
8. Subsystems are *integrated* into the system as a whole, which manifests *purposes* and *goals.*
9. Every system requires a *particular environment* for its functioning. (This is essentially the habitat concept already discussed.)

Fundamental to systems thinking is the idea of *hierarchy,* or systems within systems, organizations within organizations. In the human life, molecules are organized into cells, cells into organs, organs into the individual person, persons into groups, groups into organizations, organizations into societies. Systems theorists are seeking to elaborate principles that apply at all levels.

Miller distinguishes nineteen critical subsystems that can be identified in everything from cells to supranational organizations. The first two subsystems, *reproducer* and the *boundary,* process both matter/energy and information. Eight others deal mainly with matter/energy, nine others with information.

For psychologists, the information-transmitting subsystems are most important. It is not necessary for our purposes to explain in detail what all these subsystems do. Together they bring about the successive changes in the form of the incoming signals that they then transmit and integrate with information already in the system, finally producing the output that ends the sequence. The *decider* subsystem is, however, crucial. There must be a center where information from all subsystems is received and from which information controlling the whole system is transmitted. It may be located at more than one place and consist in a hierarchical arrangement, with final decisions

being made at the top. In the cell, the nucleus is the decider. In
the organ, a neural center performs that function. In animals,
neural and endocrine components carry the decision responsibility. In human beings, the decider is a complex, multilevel system with the cerebral cortex at its apex. In a group, the leader is
usually the decider. In an organization, a hierarchical arrangement is likely, with deciders at lower levels feeding information
to the person at the top.

Four stages are involved in a living system's decision making. The first is to establish purposes and goals. The second is to
analyze incoming information. The third is to synthesize information in a way that will limit the number of alternative actions
or outputs. The fourth is to implement the decision through
command signals to subsystems. This description sounds somewhat anthropomorphic, even militaristic, as though someone
were sitting in a tower receiving and transmitting information.
What must be remembered is that we are postulating a *function*,
not an entity of any sort. Decisions can be made by chemical
and physical means alone. Even bacteria make decisions (Young,
1978, p. 19). The fact that living systems have deciders tells us
nothing about the philosophical argument of determinism versus free will. Nonetheless, the concept of a decider as an essential subsystem is perhaps the most profound contribution Miller's
theory makes to our thinking. Purpose is inherent in life.

An open system maintains a constant stream of inputs
and outputs. The boundary serves as a filter, admitting only
some of the matter/energy and information from the surrounding environment. Note that inputs are plural, not singular—a
flow rather than an occurrence. Outputs are also plural; a person seldom makes a single, isolated response. For the psychologist, the systems orientation leads one to scan any particular research or treatment situation in which one is interested for inputs and outputs that were not anticipated when one planned
the experiment or therapy.

One important function of the boundary's filtering process is to *maintain steady states* in essential variables of the system in spite of constantly changing external conditions. Many
of these states fall under the heading of *homeostasis*, typified

by the control of internal temperature, oxygen concentration, blood composition, and a host of other physiological and biological variables. Homeostasis characterizes behavioral as well as biological systems. In fact, actions and chemical changes can be parts of the same homeostatic pattern, as when a person who becomes chilly during the night draws up into a compact solid, pulls the covers up, and finally gets up to find another blanket— all in the service of internal temperature control.

Steady state, however, is a broader concept than homeostasis. It may be a constant rate of growth, rather than a constant physical or chemical state, that is maintained. A living organism changes constantly, and control programs keep it "on track." For example, during the prenatal months and the early years, individuals maintain unique growth patterns in spite of environmental deprivations and obstacles. When a temporary setback occurs, a period of catch-up growth follows (Tanner, 1974). For example, when a newborn infant genetically programmed to be large at birth has spent its last few prenatal weeks in the womb of an undersized mother, it makes up for the imposed retardation by a period of unusually rapid growth.

Maintenance of steady states is one of the uses to which *feedback* is put. The term comes to us from the study of mathematical/physical systems involved in the technology of computers. Information from output channels is fed back into input channels for the decider to utilize. Feedback mechanisms, typified by our familiar thermostats, can be thought of as "if-then" commands. "If the column of mercury drops below the 65 mark, then throw the switch."

There are two kinds of feedback, positive and negative. The negative variety is important in maintaining steady states and equilibrium systems. It operates to eliminate or counteract the change that initiated it. Feedback indicating that there is an oversupply of sugar in the blood leads to a compensating flow of insulin. An elevated anxiety level produces feedback that leads to movement away from the source of anxiety. A consultant gives a community agency feedback on how certain policies are negatively affecting minority groups, and the information prompts the agency to modify those policies.

Positive feedback works the other way, increasing rather than reducing deviations from steady states; for example, it may generate more heat in an already overheated system. Clinical psychologists encounter many instances of positive feedback. A woman alienates her husband by a clinging overdependence on him. The more he rejects her, the stronger the dependent need becomes, and she clings to him more than ever. Positive feedback tends to produce situations that go from bad to worse. But it does have another important function: to produce *change*. It leads to the production of dissipative structures. Some things have to get worse before they can get better. In light of Prigogine's findings about the buildup of major perturbations in systems that produce completely new organizations, we can see that positive feedback plays a part in magnifying perturbations in living systems.

This brief sketch of systems theory indicates how different systems concepts are from mechanistic cause/effect principles. Systems research will require us to invent techniques different from those that psychologists have generally used in investigating perception, learning, and personality. A simple stimulus-response setup in which all variables except one are controlled cannot throw much light on the functioning of the whole complex system that is a living creature. Although many psychologists have been interested in general systems theory since its first formulation, it has not often been utilized in research. The current emphasis on ecology, however, is encouraging the consideration of systems in the planning and interpretation of research. James J. Gibson's (1979) theory of visual perception, discussed in Chapter Three, is an outstanding example of this trend. Instead of starting as most previous theories have with light rays striking the retina, Gibson weaves into a pattern everything an animal does in exploring and interpreting its visual environment.

Boundaries—Limits—Choices

As we have seen, any living system has a boundary that separates it from the surrounding environment. This boundary is not an impermeable wall confining the organism; an open system continually lets in some kinds of matter and energy, some kinds of information. It is a filter rather than a barrier. Its function is to *select* from the possibilities surrounding it. And there are *limits* to how much can be selected and utilized. In the long course of evolution or in the short life of an individual creature, possibilities once present cease to exist and other possibilities develop. Possibilities are always present, but there are always limits.

As mentioned earlier, Gould (1980) considers how structures that take shape during embryological development limit the number and variety of later structures and the functions for which they can be used. Whatever one may think about the heredity/environment controversy, it is clear that very small children seldom have the option of becoming very large adults (barring, of course, drastic hormonal intervention in the growth process, which will, in turn, impose new restrictions on possibilities). Body and brain structures developed at each stage of the life cycle impose limits on later stages.

For human beings, time is the ultimate limit constraining possibilities. Each person has only twenty-four hours each day and lives a finite number of years. And human beings are aware of possibilities they can never utilize. As William James so aptly put it, "The mind is at every stage a theater of simultaneous possibilities. Consciousness consists in the comparison of these with each other, the selection of some, and the suppression of the rest by the reinforcing and inhibiting agency of attention. . . . The mind, in short, works on the data it receives very much as a sculptor works on his block of stone. In a sense the statue stood there from eternity. But there were a thousand different ones beside it, and the sculptor alone is to thank for having extricated this one from the rest. . . . Other sculptors, other statues from the same stone! Other minds, other worlds from the same monotonous and inexpressive chaos!" (1890, Vol. 1, pp. 288-289).

Whether one wishes to or not—indeed, whether one is aware of doing so or not—one constantly *chooses* what will get through the boundary of one's own unique living system. The necessity for choice is embedded in the nature of things.

This chapter has discussed some underlying biological

principles, principles that constitute the pillars supporting any discipline that studies living creatures rather than inert matter. Psychologists must recognize the twin facts of diversity and uniqueness. They must understand the processes of adaptation and natural selection and learn to look at the habitats in which they occur. They must think in terms of complex systems rather than single, isolated variables. And they must be aware that the organisms they study constantly select and choose the material, energy, and information that they utilize from their environments. We can assume that there are multiple possibilities in every organism, every environment, every research situation, and every attempt to apply psychology in solving human problems.

CHAPTER 2

Psychology as a Science of Mind

❖ ❖ ❖ ❖ ❖ ❖ ❖ ❖ ❖ ❖ ❖ ❖

At some stage in the long march of evolution, living beings attained consciousness, and this development produced drastic qualitative changes in evolutionary processes. Biologists have no generally agreed-on theory of just how consciousness *did* develop. Philosophers and anthropologists have speculated endlessly about it; Hilgard (1980) has given a good account of the part consciousness has played in psychology since its beginning. The mind/body problem is one of the most persistent subjects in the whole history of philosophy. As Jaynes (1976, p. 2) eloquently expresses it, "Our reflections and dreams, and the imaginary conversations we have with others in which never-to-be-known-by-anyone we excuse, defend, proclaim our hopes and regrets, our futures and our pasts, all this thick fabric of fancy is so absolutely different from handable, standable, kickable reality with its trees, grass, tables, oceans, hands, stars, even brains! How is this possible? How do these ephemeral existences of our lonely experience fit into the ordered array of nature that somehow surrounds and engulfs this core of knowing?"

In the chapter containing the foregoing passage, Jaynes summarizes the principal approaches that thinkers have taken to the problem of consciousness and points out their inadequacies. Some have thought consciousness to be a property of matter itself, from the smallest subatomic particle to the most complex organism. Others have considered it a fundamental property of all living things, from ameba to human. For still others, consciousness characterizes only those organisms in which there is evidence of associative learning. Religious-minded philosophers emphasize the discontinuity between humanity and all other species, attributing consciousness only to human beings. Jaynes himself, basing his theory on archeological and literary evidence, thinks that consciousness developed in the human race only about 3,000 years ago, in the period when, for various reasons, hallucinated voices of the gods were no longer serving as dependable guides to conduct and decisions.

In psychology, during the period when behaviorism flourished, researchers tried to dispense with the concept of consciousness altogether, but as Hilgard (1980) shows, the proliferation of research on cognitive processes has brought it back into the mainstream. During recent years rapid progress has been made in relating conscious experience to brain structures. But consciousness remains a reality of our experience beyond and distinct from the brain processes underlying it. So the problem persists. At some stage of evolution, *mind* emerged, as life had emerged at an earlier stage. And psychology has once again become a science of mind as well as behavior.

Living in World 3

The philosopher Karl R. Popper proposes that we now take a further step in our thinking about mind (Popper, 1972; Popper and Eccles, 1977). Calling the physical world of reality World 1 and the subjective experience of individual persons World 2, he recommends that we designate as World 3 the mass of objective knowledge that has been acquired and perpetuated by human beings. Popper emphasizes that World 3 is autonomous, a natural *product* of the human animal, analogous to the spider's web. It does not depend on our subjective experience for its existence. The scrolls, the books, the computer tapes, the television programs, the models—all are objects in space, available for observation, study, and use in solving new problems as they occur. To quote Popper, "The third world is largely *autonomous*, even though we constantly act upon it and are acted upon by it; it is autonomous in spite of the fact that it is our product and that it has a strong feedback effect on us; that is to say, upon us *qua* inmates of the second and even of the first world" (1972, p. 112).

Popper's theory is grounded in evolutionary biology, and he devotes considerable attention to demonstrating that there is "a close analogy between the growth of knowledge and biological growth, that is, the evolution of plants and animals" (1972, p. 112). Thus, as in evolutionary theory generally, the concept of multiple possibilities has a place. There are innumerable problems, arguments, and ideas that might have been produced but have not been. Some ideas come into existence accidentally, as by-products of those the producers intended to create. Unexpected relationships between ideas newly detected by someone may give rise to "a whole new universe of possibilities, of possible new aims, and of new problems" (1972, p. 118). And as always with multiple possibilities, the richness of World 3 confronts us constantly with the necessity of selection. Any one individual can assimilate and utilize only a small part of the wealth of World 3.

The part of World 3 that Popper devotes most attention to is humankind's store of *scientific* knowledge. It consists of theories about the universe—theories that can be criticized, argued over, used as a framework for experiments, and eventually modified or superseded. Scientists are constantly changing its outlines, eliminating errors, disproving some hypotheses, leaving others standing. To *prove* a hypothesis is impossible. Absolute truth is forever unattainable. "All theories are hypotheses; all *may* be overthrown" (1972, p. 29). Through a process of facing a new problem, criticizing the currently held hypothesis about it, locating errors in the hypothesis, and reformulating the hypothesis or inventing a new one, scientists increase the supply of

knowledge available to humans. This process becomes a major
factor in evolution, facilitating a different kind of selection from
Darwinian natural selection: "Natural selection, and selection
pressure, are usually thought of as the results of a more or less violent struggle for life. With the emergence of mind, of World 3, and
of theories, this changes. We may let our theories die in our stead.
. . . Thus in bringing about the emergence of mind, and World 3,
natural selection transcends itself and its originally violent character" (Popper and Eccles, 1977, pp. 209-210).

Other creations of the human mind besides science can
also be included in World 3. The world's religions, from the
most primitive to the most advanced, are also theories about the
nature of the universe, subject to the same processes of criticism, modification, and replacement as scientific theories are.
Every culture has its World 3, although not all anthropologists
and social psychologists have concerned themselves with it.
Berry (1976, p. 50), for example, delineates three components
of a culture: (1) role diversity (economic and political), (2) so-
ciocultural stratification (social, political, family type), and (3)
socialization emphases (responsibility, obedience, self-reliance,
achievement, and the like). These components might be thought
of as a way of analyzing the *structure* of a society. But each
structure contains a vast realm of *content,* and this content constitutes World 3 for the society. There is a system of beliefs
about the origin and nature of the universe. There is often a rich
mythology. There is a body of information about weather, soil,
plants, animals, and many other aspects of the physical environment. There are moral codes that are taught and enforced. In
considering how adaptation occurs, we can differentiate three
aspects of the environment to which people must adapt—the
physical, the social, and the symbolic. Let us tentatively define
World 3 as the *symbolic environment.* Everybody, not just scientists, must adapt to it.

When we adopt this expanded definition of Popper's
World 3, certain implications become obvious. The first has
been repeatedly emphasized by scientists who study human
beings: To a large extent humans adapt through *learning.* A person must assimilate a considerable proportion of the contents of

World 3 in order to function normally, a condition not true for earthworms or seagulls—or even for chimpanzees. A second implication is that constant *selectivity* is required. We have seen how time limitations make selectivity a fundamental feature of all living creatures. For humans, the existence of mind makes this pressure very much stronger. At least in the "developed" societies, the contents of World 3 are so vast that an individual through learning can make contact with only a fraction of the total. In earlier ages and in primitive societies this problem was not so great. There was little doubt about what a child needed to learn in order to play his or her part as an adult. In our time, literacy, universal education, the prevalence of travel, and the all-embracing communications network we have woven around us have changed the picture. We cannot escape recognizing that the world created by the human mind is far vaster than anything we have experienced or can experience in a limited lifetime.

If civilization is to continue to maintain World 3, constantly increasing its scope and richness, education at all levels must ensure that every individual master some of its contents. It is not enough that children learn the skills they need to support themselves financially and handle social relationships adequately. They must also relate themselves to their symbolic environment in enough depth to be able to interact with it throughout life in productive and satisfying ways. And in each generation there must be scientists, scholars, writers, and artists to rediscover, expand, and reorganize World 3. Popper's theory about the logic of scientific discovery has been subjected to searching criticism (Lieberman, 1982), but the World 3 concept, a metaphysical rather than a logical idea, is not subject to attack. Anyone who finds it useful can adopt it.

World 3 as Habitat

Popper uses the biological concept of natural selection as an analogue for World 3 processes. Perhaps we can borrow from biology another concept that will help in comparing the world of life with the world of mind. It is possible to think of World 3 as a major determiner of humanity's *habitats.* Human beings are not as dependent on particular geographical and sociological habitats as are other forms of life. They can adapt to arctic ice, to deserts, to mountains, to jungles, to islands in the sea, surviving as one interbreeding species. What does seem essential to them, wherever they live, is a *mental habitat,* which does not depend on geography or climate, although its content may be influenced by physical variables. As happens with birds that can adapt to a very extensive geographical range, developing over time subspecies differing in structural details, so the human race in the extensive spread of World 3 habitats has developed subspecies. Mohammedans differ from Buddhists, citizens of communist countries from citizens of democracies. But they remain all one species, not only able to interbreed but able to communicate and understand one another.

The concept of World 3 as a universe of symbolic habitats can provide an added facet to be explored in cross-cultural research. To the three aspects of culture mentioned earlier (Berry, 1976) should be added a fourth—the knowledge and belief system that the members of a culture take for granted and use in thinking about the world and the people in it. In exploring how other cultures view World 3, psychologists have discovered concepts and symbols usable in our own. Jung (1964) has emphasized the importance of exploring our symbolic world.

Besides expanding the boundaries of Popper's World 3 to include symbolic creations of other cultures, we can extend its boundaries within our own society to encompass the humanities and the arts as well as the sciences. Literature, music, philosophy, history, sculpture, architecture—all the achievements of the human mind, like scientific knowledge, take on lives of their own and are perpetuated from generation to generation. They provide a great variety of mental habitats in which a great variety of human beings can live fruitful and satisfying lives. The civilized world consists not just of the two cultures Snow (1959) described but of many. There are habitats for cello players and printmakers, professors of Sanskrit and of early Roman history, Shakespeare lovers, and art collectors. To the ancient Greeks, science meant organized knowledge about the universe and human beings. Perhaps it is time for us to return to this ideal of an integrated body of knowledge made up of all the insights of scientists and philosophers, writers and artists, who by one means or another have gained such insights and expressed them in tangible, lasting form.

Inherent in this view of human civilization as a multiplicity of habitats is the necessity for *choice*. As pointed out before, human beings are subject to the same time constraints that all other living beings are. They are conceived, they are born, they grow into adults, they age, and they finally die. There is no turning the clock back, and each individual can crowd into this limited space only a fraction of the experiences possible. These limits hold for ideas as well as adventures, knowledge as well as actions. Each person must decide what is important and accept the fact that there are books that will never be read, ideas that will never be encountered, doors to new experience that must remain forever closed. But the advantage of the integrated view that we have been considering is that it enables us to find special "niches" for a far wider variety of individuals than the customary arrangements of society provide. One need not be a scientist *or* a musician, a carpenter *or* a businessman, a collector of Chinese jade *or* a climber of high mountains. In the rich diversity of World 3, one can find habitats that combine all sorts of features. But such discoveries require more thinking about priorities and limits than many people, perhaps most, care to do.

The Problem of History

The vast expanse of human knowledge we have been calling World 3 has itself a time dimension. Here, as in individual development, "time's arrow" points in one direction. Historical knowledge has some special characteristics that are important in psychological thinking. People have always been fascinated by stories about men and women who lived long before them. The story of the Trojan War and its aftermath has stimulated countless European writers. In another part of the world, Hindu people have the tales about Rama and Sita woven into the texture of their minds. History is essentially a narrative or story, and what distinguishes historians from mythmakers is attitudes and techniques to ensure that the stories they tell are true. In our century, philosophers have been puzzling over the problem of what this means. What essentially is historical knowledge, and how does it differ from scientific knowledge?

Collingwood (1965), an eminent philosopher of history, states: "Ideally, historical thought is the apprehension of a world of fact. Actually, it is the presentation by thought to itself of a world of half-ascertained fact; a world in which truth and error are at any given moment inextricably confused together. Thus the actual object of actual historical thinking is an object which is not "given" but perpetually in process of being given. To philosophize about history as if this object, as it appears at this or that moment, were the reality for which the historian is looking, is to begin at the wrong end. If there is to be a philosophy of history, it can only be a philosophical reflection on the historian's effort to attain truth, not on a truth which has not been attained" (p. 44).

Some eminent historians have tried to incorporate history into the same deterministic cause/effect framework that scientists have usually assumed. Spengler's and Toynbee's efforts to accomplish this feat are probably the most familiar. The persisting background of assumptions about "the great chain of being" discussed earlier may help to account for their efforts and for the interest they held for thinking persons. The idea that understanding the past will enable us to predict the future has great appeal. But the very nature of time makes historical prediction impossible. Danto (1965), another philosopher of history, makes it clear why it is impossible. History consists of "time-true" statements. We cannot make such a statement until enough time has passed for the event it deals with to occur. Because a prediction is a statement made before the event, it cannot be a *historical* statement. For example, the sentence "The president of the United States, Abraham Lincoln, was born on February 12, 1809" is not a historical statement. One could not have predicted that the infant born on that date would be president. Time had to pass before anyone could make what seems such an obviously true statement. It is a subtle point, but an important one, easily missed. *Two* facts are incorporated in the statement—that a person was born on a certain date and that at a later date this person was president. That those two facts can be expressed in the same statement does not give them any necessary connection. The statement is not "time-true" as Danto uses the term. "But since it is by means of narrative sentences that we ascribe historical significance to events, God, even if omniscient, cannot *know* what the significance of events is before they in fact *have* this significance" (Danto, 1965, p. 197). Time is an ineradicable component of history. Historical scholarship enables us to *add* to the truth of narratives about the past, but it can never establish their absolute truth or enable us to make true statements about the future.

This analysis of the special nature of history is important to psychologists because it is applicable to the history of an individual as well as to that of a country or civilization. Memory resembles history in many ways. We make statements about events that occurred in our lives and attempt to maximize their truth. But the significance that constitutes one aspect of this truth is not apparent until time has passed. As the significance changes, the memory itself takes on a different shape, and the statements we make about it change. One of the things that happen in the course of successful psychotherapy is that a person changes the shape of his or her memories by giving them a different significance. By realizing that there is more than one way for a parent to express love for a child, one transforms the statement "My father hated me" into "I wanted my father to show that he loved me, but he was too busy and perhaps too inhibited to do any of the things I longed for him to do." As the possibilities for reinterpretation become apparent, the rigid cause/effect link between rejection (or even abuse) as a child and neurosis as an adult that has been assumed to exist disintegrates.

The concept of *significance* is thus fundamental to psychological as well as historical thinking. And it is in connection with this concept that the habit of considering multiple possibilities becomes most essential. We cannot attach any *one* significance to events in either the past or the future, but we can consider possible significances and make choices from among them. The election of Abraham Lincoln to the presidency could not have been predicted at the time of his birth, but it could have been thought of as a possibility even then. We cannot predict precisely what any person or animal will do in the next minute or day or year, but we can think of several possible actions and plan our own actions accordingly.

Paradigms as World 3 Habitats

A book published in 1962 was to become the focus of prolonged discussion among scientists and philosophers of science. The basic thesis of Kuhn's *The Structure of Scientific Revolutions* is that the progress of science depends on two quite different sorts of process. The first sort, "normal" science, is a matter of fitting separate pieces into a structure of theory shared by the members of a scientific discipline. The second process, occurring only rarely, is the complete transformation of this structure of shared theory. To the shared structure, Kuhn attaches the label *paradigm.* He shows how, as time passes in the history of any science, more and more pieces turn up that cannot easily be fitted into the existing paradigm, and somewhere along the way a gifted scientist comes up with a new paradigm to replace the one that had been generally accepted. Such an event constitutes a scientific revolution. It happened when Lavoisier (and several others at about the same time) abandoned the phlogiston theory for the theory of chemical elements in combination. Other examples come to mind, but they are not numerous. Most of the work scientists do is "normal" science. Only occasionally do anomalies precipitate a crisis that leads to a scientific revolution.

In a later book, Kuhn (1977) explains what it was in his own development that led to this line of thinking. Beginning his career as a physicist, he was asked to prepare a set of lectures on the origins of seventeenth-century mechanics. As many historical writers do, he began with the Greeks, especially Aristotle. The usual conclusion reached in such studies is that Aristotle did not know much about mechanics, and most of what he thought he knew was wrong. But Kuhn was not satisfied to leave the matter there. Why were Aristotle's observations, so acute and accurate in other areas, so wrong when applied to motion? And why did so many people for so many years fail to detect the errors? Kuhn came to the conclusion that one must learn to read a text in a special way, adopting the whole orientation of the person who wrote it. The simple idea that made the difference in Kuhn's reading of Aristotle was the recognition that Aristotle was looking at a universe different from that of Newton and the post-Newtonians. The permanent ingredients constituting it were not material bodies but *qualities,* "which, when imposed on some portion of omnipresent neutral matter, constituted an individual material body or substance" (Kuhn, 1977, p. xii). When an object changed its position, Aristotle saw this as a qualitative change in the body itself. It would not have occurred to him to seek quantitative laws of motion.

Kuhn found that when he managed to think like an Aristotelian, the absurdities vanished, and what looked like errors from a Newtonian viewpoint were not mere observational mistakes. This realization that one could assimilate a different view of the universe enriched his subsequent study of the history of science and led to his interest in scientific revolutions as distinct from mere accretions of factual knowledge. He saw how significant for science the replacement of one paradigm by another could be.

During the two decades since the publication of Kuhn's first book, the concept of paradigm has generated confusion as well as clarity. Kuhn has tried to clear up some of this confusion in his later publications, especially in "Second Thoughts on Paradigms" (1977, chap. 12). He now interprets the concept more narrowly than he originally did, defining it in terms of the *exemplars,* or standard problems with their solutions, worked on by a scientific community. It is the perception of similarity between these problems that leads to the generalizations making up a scientific body of knowledge at any one time. What researchers consider to be "data" rests on this perception. Differences in what psychologists and astrologers consider to be data, for example, make it impossible for them to communicate very successfully. What sincere astrologers and faith healers consider to be the data on which their "science" rests are not recognized by psychologists—and vice versa.

After what Kuhn calls a scientific revolution in any of the disciplines, the similarity perceptions taught to students change, because the exemplars, or problems set for them, have changed. In psychology the predominance of measurement, statistics, and experimental designs based on statistics in the exemplars students encounter in their graduate training has produced a particular kind of research worker. During recent years, exemplars from computer technology, field observation of children and wild animals, and general systems theory have been added. Some theoreticians believe that a scientific revolution in psychology has occurred or is occurring and that, because of the mix of exemplars they now encounter, psychologists are becoming scientists who think in ways not like those of previous generations. We must remember that scientific revolutions never occur completely all at once. Galileo lived a century later than Copernicus, and during the sixteenth century both earth-centered and sun-centered astronomical theories were under consideration. Hence, it would not be strange if there were conflicting paradigms in the psychology of our time.

LeShan and Margenau (1982) argue that the whole idea of scientific "revolutions" is unsound. The restructuring of science is continual "zigzag parts of an asymptotic movement that never subsides. At any given time there is a prevalent scientific view (sometimes called a paradigm). . . . but unless the prevalent view is dogmatized, it is viscous but fluid (that is, not given up without resistance)" (p. 96). The concept that LeShan and Margenau develop in great detail is that of *alternate realities,* each requiring its own investigative techniques, its own organization, its own theories. Physicists are agreed that the questions they ask, the instruments they use, and the laws they discover are not the same for the subatomic realm, the middle range, or "see-touch" realm, and the realm of astronomical space and time. In the domains of consciousness, social science, and the arts, other realities must be dealt with. The authors build a strong case against *reductionism,* the attempt to explain one kind of reality in terms of another. Each domain must be observed and explained using concepts appropriate to it.

Can we integrate Kuhn's paradigm concept and LeShan and Margenau's alternate reality concept with the metaphor we have been using, that of habitats in World 3? Probably none of these authors would be satisfied with the integration. Their concepts differ in numerous ways from each other and from those proposed here. But they have one feature in common, the emphasis on *choice* from among multiple possible ways of organizing knowledge about the world. One of the exciting and stimulating implications of the train of thought Kuhn set in motion is not just that scientific revolutions occur from time to time but that at any one time there are different possible ways of observing nature and generating data, and one is free to adopt any one of them and to shift from one to another. The main reason we do not do this more frequently than we do is that many paradigm possibilities are likely to be invisible. The socialization process that education has put the scientist through has closed off all the rooms in the house except the one where a particular laboratory is located. Our first challenge is to open some of these doors. This cannot be done without deflecting some time and energy from the "normal" scientific activity that advances one's career, but it is a course of action open to any "normal" scientist. Instead of waiting for a genius to pull off a scientific revolution, experimenters, writers of textbooks, editors of journals, and philosophers of science can all give their minds permission to range freely over various possibilities.

From this point of view, choosing a paradigm can be seen as a choice of intellectual habitat. In adopting a particular paradigm, such as behaviorism, personal construct psychology, or psychopharmacology, one becomes a member of a group that maintains and supports the particular orientation. The psychologist's real habitat is not just the place where he or she lives and works but a community that may spread across the country or across the world. World 3 has its provinces, each with its own specialized language and culture. As time has passed, the scene has diversified more and more. Consider, for example, the great

number of new psychological journals that have come into existence in recent years. Is there any doubt that psychologists who
read and publish in the *Journal of Psycholinguistic Research,*
for example, occupy a different "ecological" niche from those
who read and publish in the *Journal of Parapsychology, Sleep,*
or *Color Research and Application?* Many such specialized
groups have formed their own divisions in the American Psychological Association. Others have set up separate organizations.
Frequent meetings facilitate communication and maintain the
identity of each of these subspecies in its own intellectual habitat.

People often make choices without realizing everything
that they involve. The thesis topics that graduate students
choose, for example, often depend more on their happening to
hold assistantships in particular laboratories than on deeply held
values. In the course of their research, however, students incorporate into their thinking the paradigms on which the research
programs are based, and they find themselves living in and
adapting to the special habitats they have entered.

To some readers what has been said may appear obvious,
unimportant, or both. But if we consider what a psychologist's
career from graduate school to retirement might be like if the
psychologist were constantly aware of the many possible intellectual habitats open to him or her, the metaphor may take on
some real utility. For one thing, it makes for an emphasis on
conscious choice rather than determination by outside forces.
Graduate students can leave programs and enter others where
the thinking of their mentors will be stimulating to their own.
This is done much less frequently than it might be if students
realized that the possibility existed. If graduate faculties were to
assume that such shifts are legitimate and desirable, they could
enlarge the opportunities for them. Even without moving from
one institution to another, within the larger, more complex departments changes of habitat can be accomplished simply by
changing from one program or one adviser to another.

At any stage of a psychologist's career, there are opportunities to try out a new set of exemplars and adopt a new paradigm. Postdoctoral appointments, short courses, and workshops

encourage this. From wherever one is located it is possible to survey a wide range of intellectual habitats by reading books and journals, going to conventions, and talking to people absorbed in different kinds of research and practice. The decision to move to another World 3 province does not even require a change of position or location, although such a change may help. One can accomplish the shift by initiating research activity of a new sort, emphasizing different things in the courses taught, or organizing new seminars and study groups in the place where one is.

It might well be that research productivity would increase if this kind of thinking became common. It is well known that, in spite of all the emphasis placed on research and the prestige and status it brings, only a small fraction of psychologists ever produce any, once their dissertations are behind them. An awareness of possible habitats might enable them to locate themselves where research would be the compelling, challenging reality it is for those who find themselves in congenial World 3 areas.

It is possible to visit for a time parts of World 3 where one does not live. Just as a sabbatical spent in a strange country with a culture very different from one's own can enrich one's thinking, so a visit to a different intellectual habitat can have profound effects. This again can be accomplished wherever one is. The process constituting such a visit is like the one Kuhn recommends for the historian of science. Just as to understand Aristotle it is necessary to think like the Greeks of Aristotle's time, so to understand Gestalt psychology one must learn to think like a Gestaltist, and to understand Skinnerian behaviorism one must learn to think like Skinner and his followers. Viewing an organized set of principles and practices as a habitat to which one can temporarily adapt promotes such thinking. The result can be a greater tolerance for divergent approaches and, even more important, modification of one's own concepts and assumptions. In Piaget's terms, one *assimilates* the culture of a different part of World 3 and *accommodates* one's own intellectual structure to the experience.

Perhaps the main difference between adaptation to a special climate or terrain and adaptation to a particular area in World 3 is that in the symbolic world the habitats exist side by side and are not visible to observers. Thus the reason for many conflicts and misunderstandings is not recognized. I do not realize that my neighbor is adapted to a different mental habitat from mine. Assumptions about human n ture and conduct that she takes for granted may be completely foreign to me. The framework of what I consider to be facts about the world and its people is not the house in which she lives.

The concept of multiple possibilities can help to elimi- nate such misunderstandings. The recognition that World 3 con- sists of an infinitely large number of possible habitats enables us to choose appropriately for ourselves and communicate mean- ingfully with others. Acceptance of our own inevitable limita- tions of knowledge and vision facilitates tolerance for the limi- tations of others and a continued search for hitherto unseen habitats we can share.

If psychology is to fulfill its promise as an organized body of knowledge about human nature and a tool for the pro- motion of human betterment, it must deal with these matters. The ideas presented in this and the preceding chapter constitute a selection from World 3 that belongs in the habitat of all psy- chologists—diversity, natural selection and adaptation, the inter- relatedness of living systems, the significance of time, the limi- tations of the individual. What weaves these strands together is the concept of multiple possibilities implying alternatives and choice. What is being proposed here is a new vantage point from which to examine all the varied activities in which psychologists are engaged. Such an examination begins with a search for *alter- native* explanations, hypotheses, and theories. In succeeding chapters I attempt such a search in several branches of psychol- ogy. Our opportunity, as members of the unique human species, to guide our conduct by conscious choices rather than accident and impulse is an inestimable asset, of which we have never yet taken full advantage.

PART II

Areas of Psychological Research Affected by the Concept of Multiple Possibilities

❖ ❖ ❖ ❖ ❖ ❖ ❖ ❖ ❖ ❖ ❖ ❖

There are several ways in which awareness of multiple possibilities can affect research in psychology. The first has been discussed in the previous chapter: An investigator has a choice with regard to paradigms and the intellectual habitats they create. Values, surroundings, life-styles, human associations, and the direction one's career takes depend to some extent on which habitat one chooses. The scientist who works in a laboratory analyzing in fine detail the anatomical structures underlying color sensations lives in a somewhat different world from the one who is studying how conflicts can be resolved in labor negotiations. In examining possible intellectual habitats one can ask questions like: How close is this field to philosophy? to physiology? How much speculation does it permit or encourage? How mathematical is the reasoning used—how much uncertainty must one live with? What kind of relationships with the people one studies does it involve? How wide or narrow is the circle of psychologists who will understand or be interested in one's research reports? How practically useful are findings likely to be? Among people working in this field, how high is the level of social consciousness? Is it the general view among scientists working in this area that researchers should attempt to use their knowledge to influence social policy or not? Although some of these questions may appear farfetched and only some of them matter to a particular person, they are really far more important for the development of a scientist than the one on which choices too often rest: Are funds available or likely to be available in the future for research of this sort?

The characteristics of one's habitat depend to a large extent on which main area of research in psychology one chooses. The world of perceptual psychologists working on time-honored problems is inhabited by people who place a high value on basic science and the pursuit of knowledge for its own sake without regard to its potential contribution to human welfare. This world overlaps that of the philosopher, on the one hand, and the physiologist, on the other. Complex instruments, which one thinks of as extensions of one's own faculties, are prominent features—tachistoscopes, oscillators, timers, recorders, and many others. Mathematics is essential; one must be able to express functional relationships in equations and fit data to curves. The subjects in one's experiments are likely to be adult human beings, usually students.

The world of the learning psychologist has some of these same features but others that are different. It is inhabited mainly by people who pride themselves on being hardheaded and skeptical. They distrust any thinking that borders on the intuitive or philosophical and prefer mechanistic models and theories. Animals are often preferred to humans as subjects in experiments.

It is unnecessary to discuss in detail the habitats of psychologists in many other fields of specialization. Anyone can analyze them by observing the daily lives of the researchers and reading their publications. Cognitive scientists and developmental psychologists associate more with workers in other disciplines. Computers have a prominent place in research on cognitive psychology, children in research on development. Social psychologists are more likely to work on problems with possible significance for human society, physiological psychologists to be located in medical schools rather than academic departments and even to take medical degrees. Enough examples have been given to show that there are multiple possibilities and to demonstrate the importance of considering habitat characteristics in making important life choices.

Within each general area of research there are far more possibilities for the choice of problems to work on and techniques to work with than are usually considered. Psychologists in the late twentieth century have faced ethical issues about choices that previous generations never thought of at all, such as the side effects of deception in social psychology and cruelty to animals in studies of learned aversions or the effects of punishment. High-level committees have been set up to develop more complex and adequate ethical codes to govern the conduct of experiments, but the most basic question of all is the one the experimenter should face before even beginning a study: Out of all the many questions there are about human nature and behavior, is this really the one I see as most important, worth the investment of large amounts of my time and talent? And among the alternative procedures I might use, are there some that raise fewer ethical questions than others?

Multiple possibilities enter into psychological research in still another way. Research designs differ in the extent to which they facilitate awareness of qualitatively different responses to the same stimulating situation. Over the hundred-year history of experimental psychology there seems to have been a drift toward designs with a narrower and narrower focus. Rather than being asked to answer a question like "What do you see?" subjects are placed in situations where they either do or do not push a button. As instrumentation and statistical processing techniques have become more and more automatic, we often lose sight of the fact that different individuals may see different things in the same situation. In the 1970s and 1980s, however, one can see signs of a reversal of this trend. Interviews with open-ended questions are coming into more general use. Mental testers have realized that some questions have more than one right answer, and theories of intelligence and personality now find a place for *divergent* thinking that leads to alternative problem solutions as well as *convergent* thinking that produces a single right answer.

Finally, there are multiple possibilities for interpretation of the data that research produces. Again and again in the history of scientific psychology, an experiment is reported as providing solid support for the theoretical hypothesis the investigator started with, only to be followed by published evidence that another hypothesis accounts equally well for the findings. In some instances, what were intended to be "crucial" experiments designed to settle the claims of two competing theories are discounted when it turns out that there is still another theoretical approach that would generate the same results.

It is such questions we shall be examining in the chapters to come. It is admitted at the outset of the discussion that research is, and must be, limited. One cannot consider all the possibilities in the choice of a field, the choice of a problem, the choice of a theory, or the choice of a means for subjects to respond to a stimulating situation. But being aware of the limitations under which one is operating can make for a broader view and may help to bring hitherto unseen alternatives to light and to generate new integrations of competing theories.

What is called into question by an emphasis on multiple possibilities is the objective so glibly stated in so many places, "to predict and control human behavior." Causality in psychology does not work so simply. There are usually several ways for different persons, or even the same person, to behave in a given situation. An observed effect may be linked to one or more of several possible causes. Any particular cause can produce several possible effects. There are signs that psychologists are beginning to recognize that complete predictability is not a valid objective for our science.

CHAPTER 3

Perception

❖ ❖ ❖ ❖ ❖ ❖ ❖ ❖ ❖ ❖ ❖ ❖

The question of how human beings and other living creatures "know" the world was being discussed by philosophers long before there was a discipline called psychology; it was the subject of some of the earliest experiments carried out in the new laboratories set up a century ago. Over the hundred years since, the nature of the experiments and of the theories they generated has changed again and again. At the beginning structuralism dominated the scene. In the United States, Titchener and his many colleagues and students built this theory on the concept of a sort of mental chemistry, in which sensations were the elements and perceptions the compounds. The theory grew out of the philosophical soil prepared by the British associationists during the seventeenth through nineteenth centuries, Hobbes, Locke, Berkeley, Hume, and Mill. Scientific psychologists took on the task of analyzing complex ideas into their elementary sensory components, just as chemists in their laboratories were analyzing the compounds into their elements. The method early psychologists used was a sophisticated kind of introspection, a way of observing one's own experience to find the elementary sensation of redness, hardness, or warmth. Both the research technique and the structuralist theory have long since been superseded, but our fund of usable knowledge about how the sense organs work and how people discriminate, perceive space and motion, judge size and distance, and carry on all their complex transactions with the environment has continued to grow.

For some time after scientific work in psychology began, a distinction was made between *sensation* and *perception*. Sensations were considered to be the raw material out of which perceptions were produced. The problem for *sensory* psychology was the nature of the relation between physical energies impinging on sense organs and the person's immediate experience of qualities like redness, sourness, or coldness. Techniques carried over from the physical sciences worked well in such research. Frequencies and intensities of stimulating energies could be measured, and Fechner and later psychophysicists were able to use these to develop measurements of the sensations as well. In vision there was clear evidence that the hue subjects experience (blue, green, yellow, and so on) depends on the frequency of the light energy, the brightness on its intensity. The retina of the eye was analyzed into its smallest units so that the units sensitive to these aspects of the stimulating energy could be identified. The electrical pathways from eye to brain were traced. Similar procedures were used in the exploration of hearing, smell, taste, and the several skin senses. For research like this it was not necessary to think about multiple possibilities. It is true that there is some variation in the responses different subjects give to the same stimulus and even in the responses given by the same subject at different times. But the variation is not large and can readily be attributed to "chance" and dealt with by averaging a number of measurements. In general, all normal subjects see "red" when wavelengths of 700 millimicrons strike their retinas. There have been competing theories about color vision, such as the long-standing difference between those proposed by Helmholtz and by Hering, but investigators assumed that as more data accumulated, it would become clear which was the right one. And that indeed has happened (Hurvich, 1981). I pass over the whole body of research on sensory psychology, even though it constitutes one of psychology's most important achievements, both because it has little relevance to the ideas I am presenting and because it could not possibly be dealt with adequately within the limitations of this chapter. Excellent recent summaries of our knowledge about the special senses are available.

The nature of the relation between sensations, the elements of the mental chemistry that associationist researchers were postulating, and perceptions, the compounds made up of those elements, was increasingly called into question as time passed, but it was the Gestalt psychologists during the first third of this century who really began to undermine the foundations of the system. They showed that we perceive directly whole configurations that cannot be analyzed into simpler units. When we listen to music, for example, the melody is not just the sum of its component notes. When we look at a picture, we immediately see shapes against a background, "figure and ground," as one of the basic Gestalt "laws" expresses it. According to the theory, the real perceptual units are forms or patterns, and brain processes are also patterned in a manner designed to produce them. We do not have to learn to perceive wholes; the process is "wired into" the organism. Gestalt "laws" provided explanations of depth and distance perception, illusions and misperceptions, as well as form perception.

Gestalt psychologists, like their predecessors, were not much interested in multiple perceptual possibilities, and their experiments were designed in such a way that all subjects gave similar reports. It was general laws, not individual experiences and performances, that interested them. But by proposing an alternative overall theory they were showing that alternative explanations of the same phenomena were possible.

During the period between the two world wars, American research on perception declined because behaviorism, the dominant theory during that period, was concerned only with overt responses, not with subjective inner processes. But perceptual research came alive again in the 1950s with the increasing influence of information theory and the realization that computer programs could constitute a new kind of model or analogue for mental processes. It is this approach that is most widely followed today, and it has proved broad enough to account for the phenomena earlier researchers had reported, as well as to bring to light new aspects of perceptual problems.

Trends in Current Research

Certain major trends that can be detected in the ways perceptual research has changed over the years fit in well with our emphasis on multiple possibilities. One of the most noticeable is the constantly increasing *complexity* of the questions asked and the answers proposed. The concept of elementary "raw" sensation has almost vanished, so that the line between sensation and perception now seems difficult if not impossible to draw. We cannot "see" a simple form without seeing also its context, the background against which it is etched. Theories of color perception, space perception, taste, smell, pain, and many other kinds of experience have had to be enlarged and amended again and again to accommodate the complexities revealed by research. Because not only environmental contexts but inner mental contexts are involved in every perception, the line between perception and cognition has also all but disappeared. The new ways of looking at mental life in our computer age have resulted in concepts that make many of the traditional boundaries between types of psychological phenomena unnecessary.

A trend related to the increasing recognition of complexity is a shift from analytic to global techniques and theories, the change the Gestalt psychologists had attempted but not quite succeeded in bringing about. Experiments are now designed to identify responses of an organized system to a whole stimulating situation rather than a limited response to a single stimulus. Furthermore, processes in time as well as instantaneous responses to situations are observed. One thinks of vision, for example, as a kind of flux rather than a series of separate retinal images.

Increasingly, also, perception and cognition have been seen to involve *activity* rather than simply the passive registration of energies stimulating sense organs and nerve cells. Gibson (1979), whose ecological theory of perception is one of the major achievements of our time, answers the question "With what does one see the world?" in this way: "We human observers take it for granted that one sees the environment with one's eyes. The eyes are the organs of vision just as the ears are the organ of hearing, the nose is the organ of smelling, the mouth is the organ of tasting, the skin is the organ of touching. The eye is considered to be an instrument of the mind, or an organ of the brain. But the truth is that each eye is positioned in a head that is in turn positioned in a trunk that is positioned on legs that maintain the posture of the trunk, head, and eyes relative to the surface of support. Vision is a whole perceptual system, not a channel of sense" (p. 205). Perception for Gibson is not just the processing of inputs from the environment. It is an active process of *information pickup*, in which the whole organism constantly explores its world for the information it needs to adapt to it. Not all present-day psychologists accept Gibson's theory, but they all place far more emphasis than older workers did on what the organism is *doing* as it perceives. For example, in a recent text, Hochberg (1978, pp. 182-183) presents "a view of perception that builds intention and attention into the heart of the perceptual process. *Perception is the active prediction and sensory testing of expected objects and events,* so that by its very nature perception is selective—by electing to test one possible expectation, it rules out many others."

This shift toward concepts of complex, global, active, selective processes in time represents a more profound change in our thinking than many psychologists realize. A situation in which an active individual endowed with a many-faceted brain, a complex muscular system, and multiple response patterns built on unique experiences faces the world is one in which multiple possibilities for action are very real. One cannot hope to discover universal "laws" of perception or design experiments in which all subjects at all times will respond in the same way. It is doubtful whether any theoretical system, however brilliant, will account for everything. As we constantly generate new data, we must expect to construct new theories.

Research on Attention

Those who study the perceptual process must all come to terms with one obvious fact. A vast amount of stimulating energy is impinging on an organism all the time, only a fraction of which can be processed by the system. Why does a person see a particular flower among thousands of other forms and colors in the field of vision? How is it that a mother hears a baby's faint cry even in a very noisy room? Questions like these demarcate the general field of research on attention—and there has been an impressive amount of it during the past century.

Dember and Warm (1979, p. 125) explain what the central problem is: "At practically every instant of our lives, the amount of stimulation available to us is incredibly large. We are showered with a plethora of sights, sounds, smells, and pressure and temperature sensations from stimuli in our external environment. At the same time, interoceptors are monitoring the positions of our bodies and parts of our bodies, and feeding us information about various tissue needs and a host of other organismic functions. Any system, physical or biological, could easily become overloaded by this vast amount of information. Because of limits to the amount of information that it can effectively process, the perceptual system must be highly selective. This selective property of perception has long been designated by the term *attention*."

Interestingly enough, researchers have not usually formulated the problem of attention in possibility terms. They have tended to assume that what a person sees, hears, or feels is *determined* by an external or internal mechanism of some sort, which it is the psychologist's task to identify. The self-evident fact that we can at any moment *choose* to perceive a different part of the surrounding complex, such as the faint ticking of a clock in the next room or pressure on the soles of our feet, has not been of much interest to psychologists. But even if research was not planned to demonstrate that one has some freedom to perceive a total stimulating situation in alternative ways, considerable evidence for this proposition has accumulated in the research findings and the theories based on them.

Some things we pay attention to are determined by circumstances. They were discovered early and have been corroborated by research at each subsequent period. Three physical factors stand out, *size, intensity,* and *motion.* Large, bright, or moving objects command attention, as advertisers are well aware. It has been suggested that this aspect of the process of attending may reflect our biological past, when survival depended on immediate perception of predators and other dangers.

There are also subjective, cognitive stimulus characteristics that pre-empt attention. These are combinations of elements that are novel, incongruous, surprising, or complex. For example, Berlyne (1966) showed that when pairs of pictures were presented to subjects, the one looked at in preference to the other was irregular or incongruous in some way, say a dog with an elephant's head or a bird with an extra head where a tail would normally be. Attention is less rigidly determined by factors like this, however, than by size, intensity, and movement, because one's past experience has something to do with what one considers incongruous or surprising. To some extent individuals are curious about different things.

It is with regard to the many internal factors related to attention that selection from multiple possible ways of perceiving becomes the central problem for research on attention. For many years, some version of the *filter* theory proposed by Broadbent (1958) formed the framework for much of the research. According to this way of thinking, information flows into the nervous system through a number of channels, assumed to be separate neurological pathways. It is the amount that can be processed at once by higher centers that is limited. Broadbent, and most other cognitive researchers, assumed that what we call memory is made up of several successive stores, often labeled *sensory register, short-term store, and long-term store.* A considerable proportion of the stimulating energy gains admittance to the short-term store but can be held there only a very short time. Between the early and the later store or stores a filter is interposed. When several messages arrive simultaneously, one is processed immediately, the others held in storage. Because information in the temporary store decays so rapidly, much of it is gone before its turn comes to pass through the filter. The flow chart representing this model is somewhat more complicated than this description suggests, but this is essentially the way it works. The filter is preset to give preference to information with the physical and psychological characteristics I have pointed out and also to information related to what the organism is seeking or trying to do.

As has so often happened in the history of psychological research, more recent findings seem less clear-cut and unambiguous than the earlier ones on which the filter theory was based. The main complication is that meaningful material does not follow precisely the same rules as nonmeaningful material like digits and nonsense syllables. When meaning is present, more of the contents of the nonattended channels appear to get through somehow. For example, at a noisy cocktail party where one is straining to catch what one's neighbor is saying, one will nevertheless perceive the mention of one's own name in another conversational group some distance away. A great many ingenious experiments have been carried out in an effort to amend filter theory to fit these complications. Other workers have gone further and attempted a reformulation of the whole problem.

The direction of this shift is suggested by the title of Kahneman's definitive book, *Attention and Effort* (1973). What is missing from all or most versions of filter theory is the *activity* of the perceiver in selecting what is to be perceived. According to Kahneman, a person must allocate a limited amount of processing resources. The effort one makes to do this can be influenced by many things, such as one's general level of arousal, the difficulty of the task one faces, the sensory modality, the amount of speededness (how fast the stimuli go by), and the fact that previous perceptual experience has made some cues dominant. The shift to a more active theory blurs still further the line between what psychologists have been calling "perception" and what they have been calling "cognition," because it involves drawing on the accumulation of information stored in the brain in order to decide what stimulus information to pay attention to. It generates concepts like *schema* and *strategy*. In Chapter Five I shall return to a more extended discussion of the emerging cognitive science. It is to be noted that research on cognition is research on what *individuals* do. Too much of the research of the past has reported some sort of average of what a whole group of subjects do. This may not correspond to what is going on in any one information-processing system. Even the term *individual* or *individual differences* seldom appears in the indexes of books on perception.

Corcoran and Jackson (1977, p. 390) make this point well in referring to a recent theory of perception (Treisman, 1969): "this theory, ingenious as it is, may represent no more than a compromise, describing the overall effects of various different strategies employed over a group of subjects, or even by a single subject from time to time. It may not explain the behavior of a single subject."

One group of experiments that did study individuals and deserves more attention than it has received was carried on by Shepard (1964) at the Bell Laboratories. The subjects were sixty employees, mostly engineers and technicians. The overall objective was to discover whether the structure of the "stimulus space" used in deciding how similar two stimuli (circles) are that differ in two dimensions (size and angle of radius) is Euclidean. The answer to this highly abstruse question was not altogether clear, but because the report presents actual distributions of responses made to each stimulus pair under each set of instructions for all sixty subjects, it is evident that individuals approach this perceptual task in different ways. Two major strategies showed up, *matching*, meaning a careful comparison of each stimulus with the standard, and *nonmatching*, meaning an overall judgment of similarity. In some of the experiments, one of the strategies was prescribed by the investigator. But when no strategy was prescribed, about half the subjects followed each strategy. There were also differences within each of the strategy subgroups. Some of the matchers matched the circles for size, others for radius angle. We need more experiments reported in this way to indicate what strategies individuals spontaneously use.

From Perceptual Possibilities to Cognitive Styles

In the late 1940s, a movement emerged in research on perception that was labeled "the new look." Following a symposium in 1949 at which a paper by Klein and Schlesinger entitled "Where Is the Perceiver in Perceptual Theory?" created quite a stir, there was for a decade or more considerable research designed to point out different ways in which individuals perceive the same stimulating situation and then to relate these perceptual differences to personality and background characteristics. One of the outgrowths of the emphasis on individual differences in perception was the concept of *cognitive style* (Goldstein and Blackman, 1978). Preliminary explorations of several of these general styles were launched and the differences they revealed given names like "leveling versus sharpening," "constricted versus flexible control," "tolerance for unrealistic experience," "equivalence range," "reflection versus impulsivity," and "strong versus weak automatization." For our purposes here it is not necessary to discuss these styles. (Those seeking more information about them can find it in Tyler, 1965, chap. 9.) During the 1960s and 1970s, research on most of these styles declined, and it somehow never had much influence on perceptual research in general. However, one of these topics took on a life of its own, and a large and rapidly increasing body of knowledge has been built on the concept of *field dependence* versus *field independence*.

This effort grew out of a series of experiments conducted by Witkin and his associates in the 1940s on the perception of the upright, using an ingenious piece of apparatus called the "tilting room—tilting chair." It consisted of a small, windowless room that could be tilted at various angles from an upright position. The subject sat inside the room in a special chair that could itself be tilted in the same direction as the room or in a different direction. On the basis of preliminary trials in which

Witkin tried out various combinations of tilts and asked subjects to report on what they felt, a standard procedure was set up (Witkin, 1949). The experimenter would set the tilt of room and chair at a certain position and have the subject manipulate controls on the chair to bring his or her body into an upright position. Witkin then measured the degree of deviation from the true upright. Fortunately, he decided to look at the distribution of error scores, not just at their average, and was struck by the fact that something other than mere inaccuracy was involved. It was apparent that the persons with large deviations from the true upright were paying exclusive or almost exclusive attention to the visual cues in the situation, ignoring the kinesthetic sensations from their own muscles. The accurate subjects were paying exclusive or almost exclusive attention to these kinesthetic cues, ignoring the visual ones. There were other individual differences as well. Some of those with large error scores were troubled and upset by their inability to carry out the task; others seemed perfectly content with the settings of the controls that they made. Subsequent experiments showed that there was a great deal of consistency in the performance of individuals at different times and at different settings and that giving them special instructions about what to attend to had little effect. It seemed that what was being detected was a major difference in direction of attention.

Two other kinds of stimulating situations were used in the Witkin experiments. One was the rod-and-frame test, in which the subject, seated in a lightproof room, looked at a luminous rod within a luminous square frame, pivoted at the center so that rod and frame could be tilted in the same or in opposite directions. The subject was asked to bring the rod to an upright position regardless of the tilt of the frame. Although in this situation the body was upright at all times, the extent to which individuals used the body as a reference could be measured by the error scores. In the rotating-room test, the person sat in a chair within a little room that could be rotated around a circular track, so that both outwardly acting centrifugal pull and the downward pull of gravity acted on the body. Here it was the people who paid primary attention to body sensations who made the large error scores. This test was infrequently used in later studies. One other test, the embedded-figures test, requiring subjects to identify simple figures embedded in complex ones, where body sensations were not relevant, was added to the family of techniques and strongly influenced the theories proposed in subsequent years. Because scores on all these tests were significantly correlated, investigators tended to assume that they were all measuring the same trait and that their job was to pinpoint more and more precisely what that trait was. It is only recently that Witkin and others have been proposing more complex theories based on a realization that the correlations obtained, though significant and often high, were far from perfect (Witkin and Goodenough, 1981).

In this attempt to organize the large amount of evidence that has accumulated, they propose that differences between individuals are based to a large extent on differences in their sense of *autonomy,* or, conversely, the extent to which they rely on external references for their perceptions. People who are relatively independent of external references are good at the cognitive restructuring required for finding simple figures embedded in complex ones and in the other situations that require "acting on the field" rather than being guided by it. They are able to separate and recombine parts of patterns and to impose organization on ambiguous material. They do well on the body adjustment tests because they attend more to their own inner stimulation than to stimulation from outside their boundaries. However, recent research has shown that less autonomous people, although they do less well on most of the tests used in the research program, are actually better at a variety of tasks involving *interpersonal* competence. They are more sensitive to social situations; they get along better with others. What is involved is a *style* rather than an *ability*. It has to do with the preferred manner of moving toward goals rather than how successfully goals are reached. Field-dependent people are more competent in some situations, field-independent people in others.

Developmental and cross-cultural research has produced some evidence pertaining to how these differences come about. It seems that individuals *learn* to attach larger weights to inner or to outer perceptual cues. As Witkin and Goodenough say, "The primary developmental investments of relatively field-dependent and field-independent people are seen as being made in different domains, so that their psychological growth is in effect channeled along different routes" (1981, p. 60). There is a wealth of evidence that such channeling does occur.

It is this that makes the concept of multiple possibilities relevant. The demonstrated fact that there are two styles, two ways of selecting stimulus information to be utilized, and that these styles have a great deal to do with the kind of personality one develops and the kind of situations to which one adapts most successfully leads to a question about how many other such developmental channels there are. It is important for research that we recognize that what is thought to be a standard experimental situation may constitute different perceptual situations for different subjects. To come to terms with this state of affairs, we shall have to use more kinds of stimulus material than we often have used in the past and pay more attention to how different individuals deal with it.

One other aspect of the most recent formulations of field-dependence theory is worthy of special notice. Because there are advantages in both the styles, it would be advantageous for a person to be able to shift from one to the other as circumstances change. Witkin suggests that some persons are in fact "mobile," manifesting the skills characteristic of field independence at one time, those characteristic of field dependence at another. If these approaches are in fact learned perceptual strategies, it would seem to be possible to master both of them. This could be true for many other kinds of perception besides perception of the upright. Perhaps the most significant and useful research on cognitive styles is still to be done.

Perception and Art

One might have expected that psychologists interested in perception would have paid special attention to artists and their public. Perception is fundamental to painters, sculptors, musicians, art collectors, and museumgoers. And it is in the complex domain of the arts that multiple possibilities are most clearly demonstrated. However, there has been very little research on the artistic experience, especially visual experience. From the time of the early structuralists on, there has been a trickle of research publications on esthetics right down to the present time, but they have never occupied a position of much importance in psychological science as a whole. (None of the books cited in this chapter except Gibson includes *art* or *esthetics* in the index.)

LeShan and Margenau's (1982) book, discussed in Chapter Two, devotes a whole chapter to this matter. Applying their concept of alternate realities, these authors call for a scientific approach to the study of the arts different from the prevailing one. They show how, in each successive art epoch, more and more possibilities became available to artists. "Each culture makes certain approaches to the infinite possible. . . . Out of the variety of coherent possibilities that exist within the limits of his cultural world-picture and the artistic inventions known to him, the artist chooses a construction of reality and writes, composes, or paints within it. The society chooses which of its artists to pay attention to, and then the artist's conception becomes a factor in shaping society" (pp. 184–185).

Toward a Comprehensive Theory

Repeatedly in the hundred-year history of perceptual and cognitive research, differences have arisen between theorists about how the experimental findings should be organized and interpreted. I mentioned earlier the conflict between the structuralists and the Gestalt theorists. There was an unsettled conflict between two theories of color vision, the Young-Helmholtz and the Hering theories, only recently resolved by Hurvich (1981). The salient conflict at the time this is being written is that between Gibson and other researchers. For most of them, the central concept is that of sense organs sensitive to particular kinds of stimulating energy, with gating mechanisms controlling the selection of what is to be processed. As we have seen in the passage quoted earlier, Gibson does not attach that much importance to sense organs; he holds that the whole organism responds directly to flow patterns in the stimulating energies themselves without the necessity for intermediate gating mechanisms. He defines *perception* as information *pickup*, not information *processing*, and uses the term *information* to mean something different from what more traditional theorists mean by it.

The challenge to perceptual theorists at this stage of history is to produce a new synthesis of ideas that seem to be in conflict. There are indications that we may be on the way to such a synthesis, through the recognition that there is more than one way to accomplish the perceptual task. A book edited by Pick and Saltzman (1978) reports the results of two workshops organized by the Committee on Cognition of the Social Science Research Council. The organizing concept is *modes* of perceiving and processing information. Modes are differentiated according to the kind of information a perceiver extracts from a situation to serve a particular purpose. Each mode is assumed to involve a different *system* made up of sense organs, neurons, and muscles. Examples of modes that have shown up in research are "speech versus nonspeech," "orientation versus identification and manipulation," "physical versus social," and "subjective versus objective." We constantly encounter such differences in our everyday experience. For example, in a crowded restaurant one can choose to listen to what someone is saying, ignoring the noisy background; to listen to what the orchestra is playing, ignoring speech as well as noise; or to concentrate on one's food, ignoring everything else. These are modes of perceiving, and people have some control over which one they use.

Pick and Saltzman (1978) point out the major ways in which this approach differs from the "classical" approach that begins with energies impinging on sense organs. Understanding perception requires the consideration of three questions, *what, how,* and *who.* Each mode imposes a different set of constraints, not only with regard to *what* information is processed, but also with regard to *how* the processing is being carried out, and the intent of the perceiver, the *who* component. Trevarthen (Pick and Saltzman, 1978, p. 108) highlights other features of the

mode concept: "At all stages action and perception remain in-
separable. In the end, however, the exploratory functions are so
powerful that they image a whole reasoned world of possibilities, a world in which abstract meanings are defined in consciousness as remote goals for projects of activity, in which the
actual component movements are undetermined until just before they are to occur. The environment of each evolutionary
form of animal is not the creator but the anticipated provider
of occasions for intelligence to flourish."

Although the concept of modes of perception holds great
promise, there is still no organized theory based on it. Different
investigators have been concerned with different aspects, as
shown by the separate chapters of Pick and Saltzman's book.
Some have focused on the "subjective versus objective" distinction, others on the "physical versus social" distinction, still others on the "speech versus nonspeech" distinction. Psychologists,
like other people, tend to think in terms of polar opposites
rather than of multiple alternatives. So far, little attention has
been paid, here as elsewhere, to individual differences. But the
basic framework for a new theoretical system has been laid
down, and a new theoretical structure that takes everything into
consideration can now be built.

Modification in Research Practices: A Summary

In this chapter I have mentioned changes in research practices that have resulted or may result from increasing awareness
of multiple possibilities in perception. Let us summarize them
here. First, the orientation toward whole ecological systems
calls for the observation of what the subjects (people or animals) do in their normal surroundings as well as in the laboratory. Such research is becoming more prevalent—and more respectable—in psychology.

Second, it seems desirable to set up experimental situations in which there are more than two courses of action the
subject may take. A great many important life decisions are not
of the "either/or" variety. We must get away from the thinking
in polarities that we find so natural. The selective attention

problem requires choices from *multiple* messages, often reaching several sense organs simultaneously.

Third, data should be analyzed for individuals, not simply merged in some sort of group average. Furthermore, the concept of individual differences must be broadened to cover qualitative as well as quantitative differences. It is not enough to show that some subjects are better than others at a research task. We need to find out also whether they are accomplishing it in the same or in different ways.

Finally, for any problem as important and broad in its scope as human perception, a wider variety of participants than are commonly used in psychological research need to be drawn in. Generalizations based on the performance of college professors and students cannot be assumed to be true of the human race in general. Research involving children and subjects from various cultures and subcultures is on the increase.

As research changes in the directions listed here, the description that has been given of the researcher's habitat seems likely to become less and less accurate. The most creative research of the future will probably be done by psychologists willing to enlarge the comfortable habitat of laboratory, classroom, and conferences to include larger segments of the world.

CHAPTER 4

Learning

❖ ❖ ❖ ❖ ❖ ❖ ❖ ❖ ❖ ❖ ❖ ❖

The question of how people and animals learn has dominated the research scene in psychology from the beginning. Learning has seemed crucially important both to the "pure" scientists who aim to discover general laws and to the "applied" scientists, the educators, reformers, and all the others who aim to improve the human condition. In this chapter we shall be considering mainly the work of psychologists of the first variety.

In this research domain there has been little recognition of multiple possibilities. Standard procedure has been to study habits and stimulus-response combinations one at a time. However, evidence keeps turning up that there are several possible ways to perceive a stimulus situation, no matter how tightly controlled, several alternative responses that can be made to the same perceived stimulus, and several alternative theories that account equally well for experimental results. It is these findings we shall be looking at in this chapter.

Rescorla (1980) has noted that there are basically three

questions to be asked with regard to any learning process: (1) What are the conditions that produce the learning? (2) What is actually learned? (3) How is that learning expressed in performance? Different psychologists have focused on different questions among these.

There are two main roads the learning researcher may take, animal research and human research, and the people who follow them differ in some respects, although they are alike in many others. Sometimes a theorist tests his or her ideas on both kinds of subjects. After psychology turned to the investigation of behavior rather than consciousness, it seemed to many psychologists that basic principles of learning were more likely to be discovered if one studied simpler behavior in animals than if one attempted to untangle the complex confusion of human learning. Controlled situations like mazes and problem boxes made it possible to observe simple stimulus-response sequences. Psychologists working with human subjects set out to design controlled situations in which they could observe other kinds of learning, such as memorizing and problem solving. The fact that the two kinds of research used different techniques and asked different questions has made the task of the learning theorist difficult. And, of course, within each of these main divisions there were specialized subdivisions, further complicating the problem of bringing all the findings together.

Animal Research

Work on animal learning, like so many other kinds of research, can be said to begin with Darwin, whose influential book *On the Origin of Species* was published in 1859. Comparative psychology was born when psychologists accepting the theory of evolution and assuming continuity between our species and its animal forebears began to examine both similarities and differences in the behavior of different species. Much of the evidence collected by early Darwinian scientists like Romanes, Hobhouse, and C. Lloyd Morgan was anecdotal, not experimental. One of the first questions to engage their attention was the relation between instinctive behavior, believed for many years to characterize lower animals, and intelligent behavior, often thought to occur only in human beings.

Comparative psychologists tended to be skeptical about the existence of any sharp line between the "animal mind" and the "human mind." The evidence they collected suggested that some form of intelligent learned behavior could be detected at all levels of life. Behavior that had always been assumed to be entirely instinctive was in fact modified and perfected through learning experiences. Pecking in chicks, for example, is an instinct, but young chicks must learn to do it efficiently. Comparative psychology got its name from the fact that its proponents actually compared the behavior of species assumed to be at different levels of evolutionary development. Individual differences within a species were also of interest, because Darwinian theory assumed that diversity makes natural selection possible.

Early in the twentieth century, animal learning research in the United States changed its direction. The objective became the discovery of universal principles applicable to *all* species. Assuming that there are such principles made it unnecessary to work with several species. One could settle on an animal convenient to maintain in the laboratory and carry out one's experiments on this species alone. The most popular laboratory animal was the rat, but dogs, cats, monkeys, and various other species were preferred by some investigators. One scientist whose work was very influential in bringing about the shift from comparative to single-species research was Pavlov. He discovered that laboratory dogs, which naturally salivated in response to food in the mouth, could learn to salivate in response to sounds or lights if such stimuli were presented with or just before the presentation of food. The concept of the *conditioned* response, as this phenomenon was called, became the foundation for a vast amount of psychological research and theory. It seemed to link up with and clarify the concept of *association* that philosophers had been discussing for centuries.

The American psychologist who did most to bring about this shift in the objectives and methods of investigating learning, drawing heavily on Pavlovian theory, was J. B. Watson, the father of behaviorism. His proposal, first enunciated clearly in 1913, became a sort of manifesto around which psychologists rallied: "Psychology as the behaviorist views it is a purely objective experimental branch of natural science. Its theoretical goal is the prediction and control of behavior. Introspection forms no essential part of its methods, nor is the scientific value of its data dependent upon . . . interpretation in terms of consciousness. . . . The time seems to have come when psychology must discard all reference to consciousness" (Watson, 1913, p. 158).

In his later writings, Watson discarded the concept of instinctive behavior, arguing that habits formed according to conditioned response principles could account for all sorts of behavior—emotions and attitudes as well as actions—in human beings and in animals. For many years this was a central article of faith for psychologists who set out to study in earnest the ways in which many kinds of behavior were initiated and maintained.

Not all learning researchers during the early years of the twentieth century were Watsonians or Pavlovians, however, and some of those who pursued independent paths are more interesting in the present context than the mainstream figures are. Among these early workers, perhaps the most influential was E. L. Thorndike (1911). He was more clearly aware of multiple possibilities in learning situations than his contemporaries or most later workers. For this reason his research reports are worth looking at in some detail. The apparatus he used most was the puzzle box, whose main feature was a rope loop hanging down somewhere inside, which, when pulled, lifted the latch on the door, thus releasing the animal from the box. Cats, which were Thorndike's preferred experimental subjects, showed a great variety of behavior when first placed in the box, clawing and biting at bars, trying to squeeze through openings, attacking the latch itself. Eventually they accidentally clawed at the loop and opened the door. On the next trial they pulled the loop sooner, and on following trials still sooner. Thorndike put them through the same routine repeatedly, observing and where possible measuring the changes from day to day. He called the process "trial and error" learning and explained it as a "stamping in" of responses that led to the "reinforcement" of escape from the box and a "stamping out" of the miscellaneous nonreinforced responses. This, like Watson's, was a completely objective theory of learning, requiring no reference to conscious experience. What the cats might have been thinking or feeling was not considered in its formulation.

Besides the diversity of initial responses, multiple behavioral possibilities showed up in several other aspects of Thorndike's work. He made a practice of recording separately the data for each subject, a practice that most later learning theorists unfortunately did not continue. He used puzzle boxes of several designs, some of them much more complex than others. Like the comparative psychologists before him, he worked with several species of animal, especially dogs and chicks, and noted species differences. (Dogs, surprisingly, were rated less "intelligent" than cats by the puzzle-box test.) And he described many sorts of behavioral differences that were qualitative rather than quantitative, things like vigor of movement, attention, and muscular skill.

In the main cat experiment, the individual differences were quite striking. Out of thirteen cats that tried all of the increasingly complex problems, three were able to solve nine of them, and one was able to solve only two. The nine others made scores somewhere in between. Furthermore, Thorndike looked at all the other things individual cats were doing (and probably learning) in the box besides pulling the loop. For Thorndike, *selection* from among various possible behaviors was the essence of the learning process. This was an emphasis that almost disappeared in later research, in which investigators with more sophisticated experimental designs and equipment made the selection themselves and tried to arrange experimental controls to ensure that only the response they wished to study could occur.

Thorndike produced a theory of learning in which a few simple laws accounted for everything animals and human beings learn. One was the law of exercise, that stimulus-response connections are strengthened by repetition. Another was the law of effect, that stimulus-response connections followed by satisfaction are strengthened and those followed by discomfort are

weakened. Later, after studying human learning more intensively, he added a law of belongingness, that stimuli and responses
belonging together are more likely to be associated than others.
The so-called law that was to have the most influence on later
thinking was the law of effect. It was another way of stating the
principle of *reinforcement,* so important in theorizing based on
conditioned response findings.

The psychologist most responsible for broadening and
deepening the concept of reinforcement and demonstrating its
utility in many kinds of learning situations in the laboratory
and in the world outside was B. F. Skinner. He proposed that in
addition to the responses to biologically relevant stimuli, such
as salivation to food, many other kinds of behavior could be
modified, eliminated, or maintained through reinforcement. He
recognized that animals are spontaneously active and that much
of this activity cannot readily be attributed to any obvious stimulus. By a long series of carefully controlled experiments, he
showed how many sorts of what appeared to be random activities could be strengthened or weakened through reinforcement.
He labeled this kind of response an *operant,* contrasting it with
the kind Pavlov had studied, in which control was simply
shifted from one stimulus to another. Skinner worked first with
laboratory rats and later with pigeons and several other species,
including human subjects. The apparatus initially used was the
Skinner box, a bare cage containing a lever that triggered the release of food into a tray. There was only one response to be
learned—touching the lever. The time it took the animal to
make contact with the lever could be measured with great accuracy and recorded mechanically. Reduction in this time score
from trial to trial, along with an increasing number of lever con-
tacts made during each trial period, constituted quantitative evidence of learning. Automatic records could be examined and
analyzed without the experimenter's ever having to make any
direct observations of what animals did in the cage. This was behavioral research par excellence, a completely objective procedure free from any taint of unobservable conscious experience.

It lent itself to multiple kinds of variation—for example,
in amount and kinds of reinforcement, in timing of reinforce-

ments, in length of interval between reinforced trials, in place-
ment of the lever, and in the amount of energy required to
manipulate it, each of which led to new generalizations about
the learning process. When Skinner turned his attention to
pigeons, pecking at a designated spot replaced lever pushing as
the response that generated the learning curves. Skinner and his
followers showed great ingenuity in thinking of equivalent
prototype responses for different species, including human
beings.

One problem that was encountered was solved early in
the history of the movement, and the solution turned out to
have considerable practical utility. The problem was what to do
about a rat that never spontaneously touched the lever or a
pigeon that never spontaneously pecked at the spot. One cannot reinforce a response that does not occur. Even in the bar-
ren environment of the Skinner box, some subjects found other
things to do instead of the designated task, and these miscellaneous activities were never used in drawing conclusions about
learning—in fact, often were never observed. The procedure the
Skinnerians came up with was called *shaping*. Partial responses
in the direction of the desired one were reinforced, and over a
series of trials, by successive approximations, the subject was
induced to do what the experimenter intended it to do. For
example, a rat in the first trial might be rewarded with a food
pellet each time it faced in the direction of the lever. After that
any movement in the direction of the lever could be reinforced
so that the rat would come closer and closer to it, touching it at
last. Psychologists interested in applying these techniques in the
training of young children were quick to see the utility of this
procedure in such areas as toilet training, for example, or the
treatment of hyperactivity. An overly active boy could be reinforced for taking his seat in the schoolroom, then for opening a
book, then for looking at the teacher, and so on, leading to the
final occurrence of the target behavior, attentive concentration
on a lesson.

As in so many fields of psychological research, the simple
elegance of the initial Skinnerian generalizations began to disappear as more and more researchers got into the act and more

and more results were reported. Skinner himself, when he began
to work with pigeons (Skinner, 1948), encountered the fact of
multiple behavioral possibilities. In an experiment on what he
labeled "superstitious" behavior, he tried to find out what
would happen if he reinforced the subjects at periodic intervals
regardless of what they were doing. Under this regimen pigeons
developed stereotyped, idiosyncratic action patterns. The action
in progress at the time the food was delivered was strengthened
enough so that the next time around it was a little more likely
than others to be in progress when the food came. This evidence
for multiplicity and diversity seems never to have affected the
generalizations about the learning process very much, however.

Psychological learning theories, like their philosophical
predecessors for centuries before, were based on the fundamental concept of *association*. It was taken for granted that complex entities are constructed from simple ones that have occurred
together. Philosophers had talked about sensations being associated to produce perceptions and ideas. Behavioristic psychologists thought that the basic entities were stimulus-response
combinations, which were associated to produce complex behaviors. During the 1920s, 1930s, and 1940s, the objective of
demonstrating that all behavior could be analyzed into stimulus-
response sequences appeared feasible to most psychologists. But
there was some dissent. Tolman (1932) and his associates came
out with a theory they called *purposive behaviorism* that differed rather sharply with the prevailing view. At that time the
preferred instrument for studies of animal learning was the
maze, and the preferred animal the rat. A hungry animal was
placed in a starting box connected to a runway that branched at
several points. Turning the wrong way at a choice point led the
subject down a blind alley. Turning the right way put it on the
true path leading to the food box. In successive trials, the rat
would make fewer and fewer wrong turns, more and more right
turns. Accurate measurements could be made of the total time
taken to reach the food box, the number of blind alleys entered, the hesitation time at each choice point, and sometimes
other variables, so that the course of the learning process could
be charted objectively without recourse to unobservable things

like memory or consciousness. Other kinds of reinforcement, such as water for thirsty rats or a receptive sex partner for a rat seeking a mate, could be substituted for food in the end box.

Tolman questioned the idea that what an animal learned in a maze was to link together a series of simple stimulus-response sequences to produce a complex response that the experimenter had decided to measure and interpret. He held that maze learning was not just learning to run through in minimum time and that reinforcement, from the animal's point of view, was not just an automatic response strengthener. In a series of learning trials, *information* about the layout of the maze and the nature of the reinforcers was accumulated to be used when needed. Tolman's work introduced cognitive variables into learning theory, concepts like purpose, plans, signals, and means-end expectations. As Rescorla and Holland (1982, p. 288) say, Tolman held "that the organism learned not just because of the reinforcers but also about the reinforcer. Tolman proposed what any layman would think to be obvious, that the learning underlying goal-directed behavior encoded the goal." What is most important for the kind of thinking I am advocating is Tolman's separation of *performance* and *learning*. In any situation an organism can be learning several things at the same time. Its performance (and that is what we measure) is a selection from possible behaviors. Most learning researchers balked at accepting Tolman's ideas because they seemed to represent a step backward toward the confusion from which behaviorism had promised to deliver us, and there were many attempts to reinterpret Tolman's research findings in ways that would preserve the basic noncognitive foundation of behaviorism. The most influential of the comprehensive theories was that of Hull (1943).

But the complications and ambiguities did not disappear. Instead, they multiplied as new questions were asked. Are Pavlovian and Skinnerian learning processes essentially the same, or are they basically two different processes (Mowrer, 1947)? How essential is *contiguity* between conditioned and unconditioned stimuli, or between operant and reinforcement? One sequence of experiments, for example, demonstrated that taste aversions could be learned even if the unpleasant consequences of food or water laced with sickness-producing substances occurred hours after it was ingested (Garcia, Ervin, and Koelling, 1966). How important for Skinnerian learning is *contingency*, meaning the occurrence of the reinforcement *only* when the targeted response occurs? As noted earlier, Skinner's "superstition" experiment seems to indicate that something is learned even when reinforcement is completely random. Other experiments (Kamin, 1969) suggested that a reinforcer is most effective when it is to some degree *surprising*, which led to a concept that what are learned are signals. This view implies cognition, not simply the automatic strengthening and weakening of responses.

The most recent attempts to put together a theory that would have a place for these and various other complications that have turned up in learning experiments make use of information theory. As stated before, the fact that computers can be stocked with inner programs controlling their behavior made it legitimate for behaviorists to assume that living creatures acquire inner structures of some sort that influence their behavior. One of the consequences of this shift away from the assumption that behavior is controlled by the stimulus is that researchers are beginning to recognize that in any situation, no matter how simple, there are multiple possibilities for learning. Rescorla and Holland (1982, p. 300) describe the change in the nature of learning theories as follows: "As important as the particular empirical and theoretical developments are, perhaps more important is the change in tone which has taken place in the study of infrahuman learning. The field has undergone a liberalization partially induced by activities in adjacent fields and reflected in the language in which theories are described. Although the field continues to demand a close tie between theory and data, as well as to emphasize simplicity and parsimony in its theories, modern views of learning see the organism as storing information about its world and deriving its performance from that information. Moreover, the organism is increasingly viewed as storing a wide variety of information and using a broad range of formats for that storage."

Human Research

Rescorla's three questions about the conditions, content, and expression of learning underlie the research on human as well as animal subjects, but the relative emphasis has been different in the two subfields. It has been easier for investigators of human learning to shift to formulations based on information processing because there has always been a great deal of attention directed to the second question: "*What* is it that is actually learned?" Human subjects typically encounter quite different situations and apparatus than rats encounter in psychological laboratories. Few of them, for example, are asked to run mazes, partly because a human maze would have to be uneconomically large and partly because the results would not tell us what we need to know about what human beings need to learn. There have been extensive efforts to study both Pavlovian and Skinnerian conditioning *principles* in the investigation of human learning, using experimental procedures specially designed to suit the human organism. These often involve verbalization.

Like animal learning research, human research grew from the soil prepared by British associationists. What seemed to require explanation was how the hundreds of tools for thinking (ideas) that the average human being has stored in his or her memory got there in the first place and how the person retrieves the ones needed for mental activity. Associationism, in either its philosophical or its experimental form, assumes that elements combine automatically in a passive organism the way chemical elements do in the natural world. As chemists do in their laboratories, psychologists attempted in theirs to analyze what the elements were and determine the conditions that led to their combinations. Early investigators decided that an analysis of how people memorized would be a good starting point, and after a decline during the heyday of strict behaviorism, it has continued as an active field of research down to the present time.

The pioneer in memory research was Ebbinghaus (1885/ 1964). He believed that to study memory scientifically, he must find some simple unit that could be counted or measured in successive learning trials. For this purpose he invented the nonsense syllable, constructed by putting together all possible three-letter combinations consisting of one of eleven vowels preceded by one of nineteen consonants and followed by one of the others. This procedure resulted in 2,300 nonsense syllables, from among which he could choose at random a list for each experiment. Ebbinghaus set up these experiments (using himself as the first subject) simply by giving the person a list to commit to memory and measuring, over a series of trials, the number of syllables the subject was able to repeat correctly. Later researchers devised another way of using nonsense syllables. They would present them in pairs and ask the subject in each trial to give one of the pair in response to the presentation of the other. Both the list and the paired-associates procedure generated numerous procedural variations as the years passed and increasingly accurate apparatus for the presentation of the syllables and the timing of the responses was invented.

Ebbinghaus and those who followed him down the nonsense syllable trail discovered many things about the memorizing process and the characteristics of the material most readily memorized. A full account of this body of knowledge is beyond the scope of this book, but some aspects will be singled out for comment. Several strategies for efficient memorizing were proposed, such as *grouping* the syllables into larger units as they were presented and *rehearsing* or reciting them between trials. It was shown that memorizing was facilitated by *meaningfulness* of the material to be memorized. (Even nonsense syllables differ in the extent to which they suggest meanings to people.) It was found that more was remembered from a series of short, spaced trials than from a single concentrated effort lasting the same total length of time. It was discovered that the forgetting process sets in and proceeds most rapidly immediately after learning has occurred. These early investigators posed but did not solve the problem of why forgetting occurs at all. Is it a simple decay process over time, or is it accounted for by interference arising from later learning? The time-honored concept of "mental discipline" was shown to be a myth. It is not true that practice in learning difficult material like Latin and Greek strengthens one's mental faculties so that learning other things becomes easier.

Thorndike (1932) was a pioneer in human as well as animal research on learning. He hoped to distill out of his many experiments of both kinds some general laws of learning that would apply to all organisms. Two laws he proposed on the basis of his animal experiments did seem to apply equally well to human learning, the law of exercise and the law of effect. What the first law means is that the more often one repeats the response to be learned, the more firmly it is established. The second law means that the rewarding or punishing consequences of one's actions influence learning. These are both common-sense ideas that most people would agree with whether or not experiments had demonstrated them. When Thorndike turned to research with human subjects, he found it necessary to formulate another law, the law of belongingness. In memory experiments, stimuli that were linked together in some way were more readily learned than those lacking such cohesion. Although this law also accords with common sense, learning researchers and theorists found it difficult to work with. "Belongingness" was a concept of a different sort from "exercise" and "effect," bringing in the subjectivity that behaviorists were trying to avoid. But the problem of meaning would not go away, and eventually it led to a reformulation of theories about how human beings and animals learn.

During several decades dominated by the work of Ebbinghaus and Thorndike, most psychologists assumed that the organism was neutral and passive, ready to process any sort of stimulation imposed on it from outside. As time passed, this assumption became harder and harder to maintain. It was found, for example, that even in learning supposedly meaningless nonsense syllables, what the subject *did* had something to do with how much was learned. People who tried to recite the syllables between trials learned more than those who did not. Researchers like Bartlett (1932), who asked subjects to memorize bigger units of meaningful material, such as stories, found that the conclusions based on nonsense syllables were not adequate to cover their results. What a person remembers of such a prose passage is a general *schema,* or mental structure representing it. Subjects could hardly ever repeat a story word for word even after a number of trials, but they could tell it and include all its essential features. The schema was a framework into which details could be fitted. Some might be dropped altogether, others amplified. Schemata used by different subjects were similar but not identical, and those reported by any one subject at different times varied in detail. More will be said about the schema concept later, as it has been taken up by other psychologists and used in the construction of learning theories of a different kind from those the behaviorists proposed.

It was in experiments where language played a part that psychologists were presented most clearly with the fact of multiple possibilities for behavior even in controlled research situations. Meanings of words and sentences are inherently multiple, and hence memorizing a verbal passage is inherently a selective process. Once this had become clear, it was recognized that selection operates even in learning less meaningful things. Take Pavlovian conditioning, for example. Early workers observed that dogs salivated in response to food and in response to light and assumed that the two salivation responses were identical. But it became apparent rather early (Zener, 1937) that this is not the case. If one looks at everything the animal does in the situation, the UR and the CR, though often similar, are by no means identical. In a later experiment (Timberlake and Grant, 1975) it was shown that when another rat is used rather than a light or sound as a conditioned stimulus just before food is presented, the subject does not bite or chew the conditioned stimulus but engages in social contact. What the experimenter intends to be a simple unitary stimulus can be experienced by subjects as a combination of multiple aspects. An animal responds to the aspect seen as most appropriate, and the response may vary from animal to animal and from time to time. On the response side, what the experimenter regards as a single unitary response can actually be a combination of separable components. Salivation is only a part of the total feeding response. The assumption that unlearned or learned responses in animals or human beings are simple, mechanical, and automatic has been largely abandoned in recent years. Meaning does matter.

As I mentioned in the discussion of perception, the major

change that is occurring is the replacement of a system of thinking based on associationistic philosophy by a different system derived from information theory. Atkinson and Shiffrin (1968) first proposed such a theory, and some variation of it is now accepted by many psychologists investigating the human learning process. Here we shall look mainly at the research on memory, turning to other aspects of learning in the next chapter. As explained in the previous chapter, it is assumed that there are several stages in the processing of information. The first, usually labeled the *sensory register,* is where large amounts of information are received and held for only a very short time. The fraction of this information that has not been lost goes next to the *short-term store,* where a small number of items can be kept for a few seconds to be coded and organized for permanent storage in the *long-term store.* (This is, of course, a very much oversimplified version of a structure that has many variations in the theories particular people have proposed.) Much of the memory research has focused on processes assumed to occur in the short-term store. In contrast with earlier concepts underlying research on conditioning, in which a passive subject automatically acquires and strengthens tendencies to respond in certain ways, theories based on information processing postulate an active subject who engages in various *strategies* to maximize the amount of information obtained. (The concept of strategy, like that of schema, will receive more attention as our discussion proceeds.) For example, in memorizing lists of words or numbers, *rehearsal* is a strategy that works for many people. Most of us have had the experience of silently repeating a telephone number over and over while we move from the directory to the dial. Many other strategies have been identified, and they constitute the basis for memory-training classes that have become popular.

The question of how information is coded in and retrieved from the long-term store has also been of great interest to researchers. A number of competing theories have emerged. The one proposed by Wickelgren (1981) is perhaps the most coherent and represents the thinking of a series of people before him. Building on a number of network models initiated by

Collins and Quillian (1969), he hypothesizes that every idea (word, number, image, and so on) is represented by a *node* in the network of the nervous system, linked in multiple ways to other nodes. This theory can account for many experimental findings, but more evidence that such networks and nodes actually exist will be needed to persuade all psychologists of its soundness. There is much still to be learned about the incredibly complex human information-processing system.

One distinction that may be extremely important in thinking about memory storage and retrieval has been pointed out by Tulving (1972). It is the distinction between *episodic* and *semantic* memory. Episodic memory is what we draw on when we try to reconstruct a conversation or report an accident. There is a wealth of evidence about how inaccurate such memories tend to be. Semantic memory has to do with such content as word meanings, grammatical rules, mathematical equations, and all the other knowledge we have for which remembering where or when it was acquired is completely irrelevant. The encoding of such information may be a different process from the encoding of isolated episodes, and there is much we still do not know about it. Such encoding is, of course, fundamental to education and to the basic task that human beings face of adapting to World 3, discussed in earlier chapters.

To discuss this problem in any detail would take us outside the realm of what has traditionally been considered learning research, into the specialized areas of psycholinguistics, concept formation, and problem-solving thinking. Active work is going on in these and related areas, some of which I shall take up in the next chapter. The more we think in terms of mental structures of some sort, the harder it is to draw a clear line between learning and thinking. There is evidence that we may be about to abandon the effort to make such distinctions and develop an inclusive *cognitive science* (Posner and Shulman, 1979).

Out of the many byways that branch out in different directions in the vast territory that learning research covers, I have chosen to traverse only a few. There is one that deserves some special attention because it is in a different direction from those we have covered, the study of the learning of human *skills*. How

does a person learn to swim, play tennis, play the violin, or fly
an airplane? As early as 1899 Bryan and Harter were studying
telegraphers, and research on other skills soon followed. It was
shown that it was important to have a series of spaced trials
rather than long practice periods and to provide the subject
with knowledge of results after each trial. During and after
World War II, psychologists working for the military were using
sophisticated instruments and statistical techniques to develop
efficient and economical ways to train workers in essential
skills. Many of the findings from these investigations and from
similar research in factories never became part of the general
knowledge that psychologists use in theorizing about learning
because those who commissioned it wished to keep it for their
own use, and it was often published in reports with limited cir-
culation rather than in psychological journals. As we move
toward a more broad-based cognitive science, it will be helpful
to bring the study of skill formation into closer alignment than
it has been with the study of memorizing and thinking. Mental
structures are involved in all of them, and the concept of strategy is similar to the concept of skill.

The use of concepts based on information processing has
made for overlap between research on perception and research
on learning. Understanding the role of attention in mental processes is important in both areas. The selective function of attention was discussed in some detail in the previous chapter.
There is another aspect that shows up over and over in research
on learning, especially the learning of skills. Attention to what
one is doing *diminishes* from trial to trial until, when the learning process is complete, performance requires no attention at
all; it is completely automatic. William James (1890) in his
chapter on habit discussed this phenomenon in some detail.
Psychologists since his time have usually not discussed it, although they may take it for granted. It would appear that selectivity decreases as automaticity increases. In the early stages of
learning a skill that requires a series of actions, such as maze
running or playing the piano, one must repeatedly select from
one's repertoire of possible responses to each successive stimulus the one that should be made. In the later stages each component action leads to the next without any selectivity.

This feature of skill learning will become more important as theorists consider *cognitive skills* (Anderson, 1981; Fischer, 1980). Designs for research may be much richer in behavioral possibilities than they have been in the past. Langley and Simon (1981) express this thought as follows: "The goal of cognitive psychology is to understand the workings of the human mind. The mind is an adaptive system whose biological function is to enable the organism to behave effectively and, hence, to survive in a complex, changing, and often unpredictable environment. ... If a system has many components, as the human cognitive system has, there may be many ways in which it can be modified, each constituting a different form of learning. Hence, it is more realistic to speak of a theory of learning *mechanisms* than *a* theory of learning" (pp. 362, 368).

Implications and Prospects

As we did at the end of the previous chapter on perception, let us look at the general directions in which animal and human research have moved over the several decades in which they have been going on. We note a movement away from the concept of passive organisms to that of active organisms, from mechanical cause/effect sequences to system principles, from automatic processing of single stimuli to selection from multiple aspects of stimuli, from actions determined by the stimulating situation to alternative performances chosen by the subject. There has been a considerable shift in psychological thinking, the magnitude of which has not yet been fully appreciated.

All these changes are producing a framework of theory compatible with the concept of multiple possibilities. Psychologists now view learning as a complex, many-faceted process. An animal's conditioned response is not a simple, automatic consequence of the pairing of an unconditioned with a conditioned stimulus, but one of several things the subject may do, depending on various aspects of the situation in which it finds itself. To quote Dickinson and Mackintosh (1978, p. 600), "Conditioning, it seems, occurs selectively in favor of better predictors of reinforcement at the expense of worse predictors; different CSs may be said to compete for association with a given US."

In other specialized areas of animal and human learning, similar evidence of response variability has shown up. What a subject does or says represents a selection from several responses that might have been made to the stimulating situation. Although many experimenters still believe that tighter controls and the measurement of more and more situational and motivational variables will eventually make precise prediction of behavior possible, it is just as reasonable to conclude that determinism is not absolute, that there is some "play" in the system, and that to some extent an individual animal or person can choose which alternative possibility to actualize.

In the next chapter we shall explore the proposed new field of cognitive science, which encompasses many things besides the work on perception and learning that we have already considered—problem solving, linguistics, logical thinking, and intelligence, among others.

CHAPTER 5

Cognitive Science

✤ ✤ ✤ ✤ ✤ ✤ ✤ ✤ ✤ ✤ ✤ ✤

In my survey of the successive periods and emphases in research on perception and learning, I could see one clear trend. More and more, investigators have been designing their experiments and interpreting their results in accordance with some variety of theory about information processing. Psychologists have been becoming increasingly concerned about *cognitive* phenomena, what the person is thinking as well as what he or she is doing. This shift in emphasis is to a large extent a movement that occurred in the 1960s and 1970s. Some would consider the landmark date to be 1960, when the Center for Cognitive Studies was established at Harvard.

Cognitive theories can be distinguished rather sharply from those they are replacing, associationism and behaviorism. First of all, they assume an *active* process of some sort, occurring in sequential phases, rather than the automatic linking of contiguous ideas or stimuli. Second, they postulate mental *structures* of some sort that impose form on input and control output. Third, they merge lines of research that have traditionally been separate, perception, memory, learning of skills, problem solving, and various others, incorporating the findings of experiments in these separate fields in their more inclusive formulations. Even things we have customarily classified as affective or motivational phenomena, such as intentions, desires, beliefs, and values, are being included in the new theories, and the distinction between cognition and motivation is becoming blurred. Finally, many theorists are emphasizing the *interdisciplinary* aspects of the new cognitive science. Linguistics has played an important part in its development. So has computer engineering.

In fact, it was the growth of computer technology that made a different sort of psychological research possible. Down through the centuries in which psychology has existed as a separate discipline, there have been theorists who proposed ideas similar to those that make up the cognitive theories, but because there seemed to be no way of testing them scientifically, their influence declined. Psychologists have always emphasized scientific values and attempted to anchor their theoretical concepts to *observable* variables. Because thoughts, intentions, and feelings are not directly observable, hardheaded theorists preferred to base their explanations on the manipulation of stimuli and the observation of responses, without speculating about what might be going on inside the organism. Computer technology made it possible to include inner states in an unquestionably scientific explanation. The new concepts were more complex than those they replaced. "Input" replaced "stimulus"; "output" replaced "response." And between the two was a series of happenings controlled by a "program." The concept of an interactive *system* replaced that of cause/effect linkages between single variables. Psychologists could now talk about mental processes without abandoning their scientific principles.

As mentioned above, it was soon realized that others besides psychologists had been doing research on the same processes. Philosophers were adapting their thinking to the new concepts. Linguistics underwent a period of very rapid development during the middle decades of the twentieth century. Neurologists were finding the systems concepts very useful. Creative engineers set themselves the task of *simulating* electronically the unobservable cognitive realities the others were trying to infer. It is because of this union of several disciplines that some workers now advocate replacing the label *cognitive psychology* with *cognitive science* (Posner and Shulman, 1979).

Two main approaches to research on cognition can be distinguished. One is a continuation of experimental work in psychology, using the new concepts to make the experiments more productive. Posner and McLeod (1982, p. 478) state that this approach is based on an assumption that "detailed studies of particular configurations will lead to the identification of fundamental operations that can be used to characterize the human mind." One might call this a "bottom-up" strategy for building cognitive theory. The other main approach, most clearly represented by Simon (1981), is to design artificial systems to carry out activities for which we have always considered human intelligence essential and use our understanding of how these artificial systems work to help us understand how human minds may work. It might be labeled a "top-down" strategy. Both approaches have brought notable successes; both have limitations. I shall take them up separately.

"Bottom-Up" Research: Psychological Research

Some work of this sort has already been reported in previous chapters on perception and learning, but its scope is much broader than these two topics, and it no longer seems useful to separate perception, attention, memory, thinking, and learning, as has been customary in psychology and philosophy. In the new, more inclusive study of cognition, Posner and Shulman (1979) distinguish four main topics: (1) Representation. How is it that the mind is able to represent a concrete object (for example, apple) or an abstract concept (for example, justice) in the absence of current sensory stimulation? (2) Laws or rules of thought. Do people tend to follow the normative prescriptions of logic, even though often unsuccessfully, or are they subject to some definable "psycho-logic"? (3) Products of the thought processes that emerge during problem solving. For example, how do chess masters represent the pieces of the game in their position on the board after each move in a way that allows them to decide on the next move? (4) Individual differences in cognitive abilities. What sorts of differences in cognitive processes account for the marked differences in people revealed by intelligence tests?

As a vehicle for exploring the cognitive terrain, psychologists have been using a method called mental chronometry, proposed by Donders in 1868 but not really exploited until a century later. It involves the measurement of reaction time under different conditions that require subjects to use different parts of their total cognitive equipment. It is hypothesized that when the instructions make it necessary for the person to use an extra part of the system, the time it takes to respond will increase accordingly. By analyzing these time records, the investigator can make inferences about what is going on in the subject's mind. For example, a subject may be asked to press a key as soon as a light comes on, and the reaction time is measured. Then the instructions will be changed, and the subject will be asked to press one of two keys, the first if a red light comes on, the second if a green light comes on. The second condition involves a choice or decision in addition to the process involved in the first condition. One would expect that this would increase the time needed for the response, and indeed, the times do turn out to be significantly longer. Other tasks that require the subject to retrieve information from long-term memory take still longer. By subtracting the shorter from the longer times, psychologists can draw tentative conclusions about the nature and relative importance of various cognitive subsystems. Posner and McLeod (1982) view mental chronometry as "a set of tools that can be aids in the decomposition of performance into sets of internal operations" (p. 484).

One of the most important ideas that psychologists have picked up from computer technology is that of *coding*. Much of the work on the first of the major tasks listed by Posner and Shulman, the problem of representation, can be thought of as an effort to find out how information is coded in the human cognitive system. Here researchers have run into the fact of multiple possibilities once more. There seems to be more than one way to code. Bruner, Oliver, and Greenfield (1966) proposed that we think of three main kinds of codes—iconic, symbolic, and enactive. Iconic codes are images, and some information is undoubtedly stored in such mental pictures. Symbolic codes are words and numbers and the structures built from them, such as phrases and equations. Enactive codes organize a sequence of movements into smoothly functioning actions. The whole problem of knowledge representation is much more complex than this. Some of the complications will be considered in later sections. But a consensus seems to be emerging that no single theoretical system will account for all the findings about how human beings store and retrieve information. We must learn to think in terms of repertoires of coding skills available for use under different circumstances.

Psychologists following "bottom-up" strategies have contributed less to the study of Posner and Shulman's second and third questions than have the "top-down" investigators to be considered in the next section. But they have made a beginning on the fourth, the study of individual differences. There are, of course, many ways in which one person's cognitive structures and processes could differ from another's. So far much of the effort has gone into finding out whether measurements of some of the partial processes by mental chronometry are related to what is measured by intelligence tests. Hunt and Lansman (1975) have summarized some of this work. They report, for example, that differences in the time taken for initial coding are related to differences between students in the top quarter and students in the bottom quarter of the intelligence distribution. The time taken to retrieve information from long-term memory is also correlated with scores on reading comprehension, according to Hunt, Davidson, and Lansman (1981). Jensen (1980) found differences between retardates and normals on several aspects of reaction time. Research on information processing has also reawakened interest in an old problem that goes back to the early years of psychology's history, the distinction between visualizer and verbalizer types (Snyder, 1972). So far none of the findings from these excursions into the territory of individual differences has been very impressive. Correlations are low even when significant, and differences between contrasting groups are not large. Perhaps in the long run the demonstration that there are individual differences in the techniques people use to process information will contribute more to education than a demonstration that such differences correlate with mental measurements would contribute. And cognitive science may bring together the two disciplines of scientific psychology that Cronbach (1957) talked about, experimental and correlational psychology, as well as break down the barriers that have separated social, developmental, personality, and motivational psychology from experimental, physiological, and mathematical specialties.

"Top-Down" Research: The Impact of the Computer

During recent decades, something genuinely new has been added to our resources for understanding how the human mind works. The whole undertaking often goes under the label of *artificial intelligence* (AI), and it is still a somewhat controversial topic among psychologists and philosophers. The general plan of such research is to design a computer that will carry out some task for which human intelligence was heretofore thought essential and then to use one's understanding of the processes through which the computer accomplished the task as a source of hypotheses about how human intelligence accomplishes it. Perhaps the most successful product of AI research so far is the electronic chess player. It can beat most human players, although grand masters of the game can usually defeat it. The chess-playing program can stand as a prototype of what research on artificial intelligence is about. And it has already led to new insights about memory and problem solving.

Not all AI researchers subscribe to the entirety of the foregoing statement of purpose. Many engineers and computer scientists are simply seeking efficient ways to solve problems and are not really interested in the question whether the human mind solves them in the same way. Many useful techniques have come out of "think tanks" and research institutes, techniques that are being applied in military strategy, weather prediction, urban planning, and other special fields. But for psychologists it is the analogy with human functioning that is most intriguing.

Before going into more detail about this research, we should be clear about its limitations. We should realize that no matter how well a computer solves a problem or plays a game, we can never conclude, "This *is* the way the brain does it." It is necessary to do further research using psychological techniques to pin down any psychological conclusion. But this very fact is what makes the AI movement of particular interest to us in thinking about multiple possibilities. In two complex systems, the fact that the two inputs and the two outputs are identical does not prove that what goes on in between is identical. Different processes can produce the same result, and if this is true in comparing computers with brains, might it not also be true that two brains achieving the same solution to a problem need not have functioned in the same way?

It was perhaps unfortunate for public understanding that the term *computer* was used as a label for information-processing machines and that their first wide-scale use was for the rapid processing of *numerical* data. Essentially, what the computer is (Haugeland, 1981) is a *formal system,* "a game in which tokens are manipulated according to rules in order to see what configurations can be obtained" (pp. 5-6). A *digital* formal system has three essential properties. (We shall not be concerned here with the other variety, analogue systems, as they have been much less frequently used in the research we are considering.) These properties are:

1. The system is entirely self-contained.
2. Every relevant feature of the game being played with tokens and rules is perfectly definite. The only answers are "Yes" or "No," 1 or 0.
3. Every move is *finitely checkable* to see whether it is legal given the tokens and the rules.

A computer is an *automatic* formal system programmed, or preset, to manipulate the tokens according to the rules. The ancestor of all of them was the Turing machine, invented by the mathematician Alan Turing in 1937. In the abstract, it consisted of three essential parts: first, an unlimited number of storage bins, each of which could contain only one formal token at a time; second, a finite number of execution units, or rules for moves; and third, one indicator unit to record the current state of the system and show what move should be made next. (For a complete description, see Haugeland, 1981, pp. 10–15.)

In the simplest automatic systems there is never any doubt about the move that should be made next. But in the more complex systems where the analogies to human intelligence are sought, there are usually several moves that would be legal in each successive condition, and the question is "Which one?" The necessity of choosing between alternatives is what is called the control problem, and the built-in procedures for handling it are *production systems*. What the computer must do is to search for and examine the consequences of each possible move as a basis for choosing one of them. Because of the speed at which it operates, the computer can carry out such a search very rapidly. But it soon became apparent in AI research that in solving all but the simplest problems there were just too many alternatives for a complete search to be feasible. Consider the chess player, for example. In the average position of the pieces on the board, Haugeland estimates that a player will have thirty to thirty-five legal possibilities for the next move. To evaluate each, one should consider all the sequences of moves in the remainder of the game to which this move might lead. In a typical game of forty moves, the number of possible sequences turns out to be 10^{120}, many times more than the number of seconds since the beginning of the universe, according to Haugeland (p. 26). A chess player, human or machine, obviously does not do this. What it must be designed to do is to select only *relevant* possibilities and ignore the rest. Most of the thirty or more legal options would be pointless or stupid. Procedures a computer uses in selecting relevant possibilities are called *heuristics*. These can be thought of as policies guiding search. They are not foolproof and are more like rules of thumb than like logical rules. For example, one chess heuristic might be "Never trade a queen for a pawn." One of the first breakthroughs in AI research was the designing of the General Problem Solver (Newell,

Shaw, and Simon, 1958), incorporating in its makeup a number of heuristics.

The next step forward came when researchers turned their attention to types of problems whose solutions require not only problem-solving *skills* but a considerable background of *knowledge*. The tokens used in such formal systems have meanings that relate them to the outside world. This is where linguistics becomes an important ingredient of AI research. The theory of meanings is called *semantics*; the formal aspect of a linguistic system is called *syntax*. Both aspects and the relationship between them are of great concern to those seeking solutions to real-world problems.

In the years before information processing became the dominant theory, psychological research on memory, on the learning of skills, and on problem-solving thinking were often completely separate areas, using different techniques, publishing in different journals—in short, occupying different World 3 habitats. Investigators following the AI path have brought them together. They see them as involving two different kinds of knowledge, declarative and procedural. *Declarative* knowledge is the accumulation of facts we have learned, organized into *schemata,* which are large, complex units representing whole categories of objects, people, and events. Much of the material one learns in school and most of the miscellaneous information one picks up from other people, newspapers, radio, and television is of the declarative sort. *Procedural* knowledge, in contrast, consists of sequences of representations of actions we have learned to perform. It is stored as production systems. These can be described as rules of the "if-then" variety, a linkage of a condition with an action. Anderson (1980, p. 239) gives as an example of one of these procedural units:

> IF a car is in first gear
>   and the car is going faster than ten miles an hour
>   and there is a clutch
>   and there is a stick
> THEN depress the clutch
>   and move the stick to the upper right position
>   and release the clutch.

(Obviously this system applies to a three-speed car.) When a skill has been so well learned that it requires no investment of attention, the whole process runs off automatically and very quickly.

Everything psychologists have found out about long-term memory is relevant to the storage of both kinds of knowledge. As explained earlier, the way to increase the amount of information that can be processed at one time is to combine a number of units into a single unit, the process of *chunking*. Individuals develop highly idiosyncratic bases for chunking, some of them remarkably effective. Chase and Ericsson (1981), for example, report a study on an undergraduate with only average intelligence and an average memory span who was paid by the hour to take part in a psychological experiment. For about an hour a day, two to five days a week, he listened to a list of digits and tried to recall as many of them as possible. At the end of each trial he reported on the mental processes he had used. During the twenty-five months the experiment lasted, he increased his digit span from seven to fifty digits. His verbal reports showed that his method was to combine several digits into a figure that he remembered as a running time for some standard distance. One group of digits, for example, would be remembered as "very poor mile time," another as "average time for the marathon." He would then arrange the times for each category in order—the one-mile times, the two-mile times, and the times for various shorter and longer distances. The few digits he was unable to fit into this system were chunked in some other way. The set 896 was remembered as 89.6, a very old man; 1943 was remembered as near the end of World War II. The case is an impressive demonstration of how knowledge can be organized. It goes without saying that only a person enthusiastic about running could use this system, and he or she could use it only for digits, not for words or sentences. But it reminds us of the multiplicity of possibilities that exist here. Probably any one of us has knowledge based on experience of some special sort that could serve as a framework for storing new knowledge. To return to our chess-playing example, Chase and Simon (1973) discovered that what distinguishes the master from the amateur is the information held in long-term memory about the positions of pieces on the board. At any stage of the game, the master looks at the board and perceives not a lot of separate pieces but a few major configurations. For each of these he remembers the organized sequences of moves likely to follow it.

Probably the most accepted psychological theories about how information is stored postulate a sort of *network* with multiple *nodes,* each connected with many other nodes (Wickelgren, 1981). Research that psychologists down through the years have done on concept learning provides clues to how this network is acquired. Concepts can be thought of as coding systems that can be used in assigning new information to its appropriate place in the network. Although concepts may not be the only kind of nodes in the network, what we know about them can help us understand the whole system. There are basically two kinds of links between concepts, one involving a "superordinate-subordinate" relationship, such as "animal—dog," and the other a "same-level" relationship, such as "dog—cat." Collins and Quillian (1969) proposed that the network of memory is a hierarchy with several levels of abstraction—for example, "canary—bird—animal—living thing." Properties such as "yellow," "has wings," "breathes air," or "reproduces itself" are linked horizontally to concepts at the different levels. These investigators designed some ingenious chronometric experiments to test the theory, and although these were not absolutely conclusive, they were persuasive. Many other experiments have produced results compatible with this sort of network theory. There are other theories. Schank and Abelson (1977), for example, hold that the basic units of organization are *episodes.* People encode and retrieve knowledge in *scripts* covering particular episodes and *plans* for putting together disconnected units and making sense of them. There seems to be little point in arguing about which theory is right. People may use both concepts and scripts and perhaps other organizing principles as well. In separate chapters of Haugeland's edited volume (1981), Dreyfus discusses scripts, and Minsky discusses scenarios and frames.

The psychology of language has become very important

in the attempt to simulate mental processes that use meaningful material. At the end of his introductory chapter, Haugeland (1981, p. 31) restates the basic premise of cognitive science, that *"intelligent beings are semantic engines—*in other words, they are automatic formal systems with interpretations under which they consistently make sense." He also faces the possibility that the premise itself may be wrong—that people are not semantic engines. In several later chapters of the book, some writers talk about the limitations of cognitive science, particularly the research on artificial intelligence. But others are more optimistic about its prospects (Newell and Simon, 1981). Fortunately, a psychologist does not need to be a "true believer" to make use of whatever insights this line of research has to offer.

AI Research on Problem Solving

One of the clearest and most thorough accounts of what has been accomplished is Simon's *Sciences of the Artificial,* second edition (1981). Simon summarizes the history of the movement and proposes some ideas of his own, ideas that are worth considering whatever our final judgment of research on artificial intelligence may be. He believes that there has come into existence a new *science of design,* which may be of the utmost importance in human affairs. His basic contention is that such professional specialties as engineering, architecture, medicine, law, and business should not be thought of as applied science, as they are generally. In our present academic culture, engineering schools have become schools of physics and mathematics; medical schools have become schools of biological science; business schools have become schools of economics and finite mathematics. Simon would like to change this.

Design science differs from "pure" science in several ways. It rests on a different logic because it is concerned with how things "ought to be" rather than how things "are." It requires an imperative rather than a declarative logic. Because its objective is to devise artifacts to attain human goals, *intentionality* is an essential attribute. In this limited, technical use of the word *intentionality,* "a particular thing is an intentional system only in relation to the strategies of someone who is trying to explain and predict its behavior" (Dennett, 1981, p. 221). The design scientist must constantly choose from alternatives. Hence, an activity always involved is *search,* the search for alternatives. Design science also has to do with *limitations* of many sorts, such as time, money, and energy. The search process and the final choice are controlled to some extent by awareness of these limitations. Only feasible alternatives need be considered.

Statistical decision theory is a branch of mathematics used as a means of *optimizing* choices. Widely applied in economics and in engineering, it has spread to many other disciplines and situations in which one must choose a course of action to produce the greatest benefit at the least cost. Simon makes an extremely important suggestion for modifying decision theory, recommending that the objective of the search process be *satisficing* rather than optimizing. Finding the best possible alternative can be a prolonged if not impossible undertaking. Simon explains his new idea this way: "An earmark of all these situations in which we satisfice for inability to optimize is that, although the set of available alternatives is 'given' in a certain abstract sense (we can define a generator guaranteed to generate all of them eventually) it is not 'given' in the only sense that is practically relevant. We cannot within practicable computational limits generate all the admissible alternatives and compare their respective merits. Nor can we recognize the best alternative, even if we are fortunate enough to generate it early, until we have seen all of them. We satisfice by looking for alternatives in such a way that we can generally find an acceptable one after only moderate search" (p. 139).

This limited search process was built into the computer model for problem solving (GPS) that Newell and Simon designed. It required that one set up at the outset criteria for an acceptable alternative. As soon as an alternative turns up that meets these criteria, the search stops. As might be expected, doing this involves many complications, and Simon explains in detail how some of them are dealt with.

One technique is to decompose the complete design into functional components and deal with these separately. This recommendation leads Simon to a discussion of another concept that is crucial in his thinking and in that of most systems theorists, the concept of *hierarchy*. We have already seen how it is used in theories about memory storage. The word *hierarchy* as used by systems theorists does not mean quite the same thing as it does in common speech, because it carries no implication that there is any authority relationship between systems at higher and lower levels, as, for example, in the ecclesiastical hierarchy, where bishops exercise authority over priests, archbishops over bishops, and so on. Higher-level systems do not control subsystems, which are almost but not quite independent both of higher systems and of other systems at the same level. In Simon's *nearly decomposable* systems, this independence prevails in the short run, but in the long run the aggregate effects of the components interact. As a simple example of what he means, Simon asks us to think of a building divided into rooms, each room containing a number of cubicles. The outside walls of the building are insulated so well that they provide perfect protection against the thermal environment. The walls of the rooms are also insulated, but not perfectly. Some heat can leak through. The walls of the cubicles are not insulated at all. When we first observe the system and subsystems, there is a wide variation in temperature from cubicle to cubicle and some variation from room to room. What happens when we take temperature readings several hours later? The differences between cubicles have completely disappeared, but there is still some difference from room to room. If we come back a week later, we will find that the room-to-room differences have also disappeared; the whole inside of the building now has the same temperature. Heat transfer is a dynamic process, and Simon analyzes the differences between systems at different levels of complexity in dynamic terms.

The main reason that decomposing a complex system into subsystems is so useful in AI research is that there is a great deal of *redundancy* in complex structures. There can be a large number of subsystems but only a few *types*. It is only the aggregate properties of these types that interact to produce the complex system. Thus, by analyzing the interactions of a limited number of systems simple enough to be readily analyzed, we can make inferences about the structure of the whole. "One way to solve a complex problem is to reduce it to a problem already solved—to show what steps lead from the earlier solution to a solution of the new problem. If around the turn of the century we wanted to instruct a workman to make an automobile, perhaps the simplest way would have been to tell him how to modify a wagon by removing the singletree and adding a motor and transmission. Similarly a genetic program could be altered in the course of evolution by adding new processes that would modify a simpler form into a complex one—to construct a gastrula, take a blastula and alter it" (p. 226). In order to use this strategy for understanding a complex system, the first thing one must do is to represent or describe it in a way that brings the subsystems into view. "How complex or simple a structure is depends critically upon the way in which we describe it. Most of the complex structures found in the world are enormously redundant, and we can use this redundancy to simplify their description. But to use it, to achieve the simplification, we must first find the right representation" (p. 228).

Of all the workers who have labored in the field of artificial intelligence, Simon is perhaps the most profound. The three ideas that have been presented here are major contributions to cognitive science, whatever shape it eventually takes—*design*, having to do with the purpose of the whole undertaking, *satisficing*, having to do with the techniques used, and *hierarchy*, the idea that anchors the research to general systems theory.

It begins to look as though *artificial creativity* would be a more suitable label than *artificial intelligence* for the computer-based research. The term *intelligence* has been used mainly in connection with individual differences showing up on tests that measure the overall quality or complexity of the thinking people do. There have been some attempts to bring the work of mental testers and cognitive researchers into alignment (Resnick, 1976), but the bulk of the AI research has little to do with intelligence as we measure it. It does tie in with an idea proposed by Guilford (1950) in a paper on creativity—namely, that there is a clear distinction between *convergent* and *divergent* thinking. Convergent thinking is the kind we use in solving problems for which there is only one correct answer. Divergent thinking is used in dealing with problems for which a variety of solutions can be generated. Intelligence tests measure convergent thinking almost entirely. But divergent thinking seems more similar to what computer simulations do, especially if Simon's concept of satisficing rather than optimizing is adopted.

Thinking about creativity brings us back to Simon's concept of design science, which may well be the most significant contribution cognitive science has yet made to human progress. As Simon puts it, "The proper study of mankind has been said to be man. . . . If I have made my case, then we can conclude that, in large part, the proper study of mankind is the science of design, not only as the professional component of a technical education but as a core discipline for every liberally educated person" (p. 159).

Cognitive Science and Multiple Possibilities

Even though it is still in its beginning stages, more interesting for what it promises than for what it has accomplished, research on cognitive science has been emphasized here because it exemplifies the new orientation presented in this book. Psychologists working in this area have made the shift from unity to multiplicity, from the quest for certainty to the acceptance of uncertainty, from the prediction of single events to the exploration of the consequences of several alternatives, from linear relationships to systems.

In the writing that is being done about cognitive science one finds many examples of this shift. First of all, researchers recognize that many different processes may link identical inputs to identical outputs. Second, heuristic search involves alternative actions and, if we adopt a satisficing objective, alternative outcomes as well. Optimizing is inherently singular; satisficing is plural. Third, when we consider the part that stored knowledge plays in thinking by human or machine, it becomes apparent that information can be coded for storage in more than one way. If memory is a network of nodes and links, there must be multiple links for each node and multiple ways in which ideas can be associated.

This is especially true for ideas expressed, as they usually are, in language. A word or a sentence has multiple meanings, and each person means something a little different than the next person does by the words he or she uses. This is because each person is shaped by a unique set of experiences leading to a unique set of beliefs, attitudes, and expectations. Davidson (1981) makes the point that to come to a full comprehension of what someone means, we must have some understanding or at least hypothesis about what he or she *might* have said under the circumstances. Such an inventory of possibilities is not made consciously or thoroughly, of course, but the process is one we can recognize that we do carry on, and it is an aspect of linguistic communication that should not be ignored. When we consider problems of how learning occurs and how cognitive systems change over time, multiple possibilities are again in evidence. As Simon (1981, p. 118) puts it, "Any multicomponent system can be improved in a large number of ways. Nor is there any single kind of change in the human cognitive system to which the term *learning* applies exclusively."

Other examples could be given. Perhaps the most important result of what some have called the "cognitive revolution" is that we are finding out that there is more than one way to be scientific. The assumptions most psychologists have made in the past, that the hypotheticodeductive method is the only one permissible and that complex phenomena of life and mind are ultimately to be explained in terms of physical and chemical principles, are too restrictive to characterize all of science. Haugeland (1981, p. 244) has this to say about the matter: "Science itself often leaves behind efforts to say what it can and cannot be. The cognitive approach to psychology offers, I think, a science of a distinctive form and thereby sidesteps many philosophical objections—including those born of a dazzled preoccupation with physics."

CHAPTER 6

Social Psychology

❖ ❖ ❖ ❖ ❖ ❖ ❖ ❖ ❖ ❖ ❖ ❖

Such branches of psychology as personality, developmental, and social are often spoken of as "soft" rather than "hard" science. In these areas it has been more difficult to apply the concepts and techniques of the physical sciences, and attempts to "predict and control" have fallen far short of success. I shall examine in some detail the problems that have arisen and the kinds of solutions that have been proposed in social psychology.

Psychologists have usually defined this area as the study of the individual's responses to social stimulation. Not all workers who call themselves social psychologists accept this definition, however. There have always been two contrary conceptions of what was to be studied, often finding expression in two different college courses, one taught by psychologists, the other by sociologists. Sociologists are inclined to ascribe some sort of reality to groups themselves, beyond a summation of the responses of individual members. Even the founder of experimental psychology, Wilhelm Wundt, believed that there was some sort of entity as a group mind and that it could not be investigated by the analytic techniques he was using in research on individuals. Many social philosophers and social scientists have postulated a group mind over and beyond the individual minds of group members. What lends them some cogency is the fact that individuals in social groups are not just responders. They continually emit stimuli as well as responses, and this *interaction* is fundamental to social reality. As general systems theory replaces stimulus-response theory, it becomes easier to conceptualize problems in this way.

The idea of considering multiple possibilities is especially relevant in social psychology because there is an inherent multiplicity about social situations. Words have several meanings; gestures are often ambiguous; feelings are complex and wear various disguises. There is more than one way to respond to any combination of social stimuli. In social interaction one is always making choices about what something means and what one should say or do. This is one of the reasons for the "softness" of the science. Techniques worked out to control variables in experiments on color vision or the learning of a skill turn out to be inadequate controls in social situations. There are just too many extraneous variables, and we may not even be aware of many of them. Thus, much research in social psychology has been informative but not definitive. Until about 1920, books such as McDougall's (1908) presented theories based on general observation rather than research findings. A change of direction was initiated by F. H. Allport (1924), who set out to construct a social psychology grounded in learning theory.

Four kinds of problems have engaged the attention of researchers (Steiner, 1979). First, how are attitudes, which many psychologists considered the basic motivating forces, developed and changed? Second, how does the presence of other people influence the individual's performance for better or worse on various experimental tasks? Third, how does group performance on problem-solving tasks compare with individual performance? Fourth, how do people perceive or infer one another's feelings, motives, and personality characteristics?

Research on these questions during the 1920s and 1930s

fell short of being fully scientific by the standards being set up by investigators in other areas. It was usually done in classrooms and other natural settings, using as subjects people who happened to be available at the time. Thus, the criterion of representativeness basic to statistical analyses of data was not met, and there was always some uncertainty about how far the conclusions could be generalized. The fact that many of the variables were not under the experimenter's control was another source of uncertainty about the conclusions. Social psychologists had to be content with tentative conclusions, which took on more credibility if they were confirmed, as they often were, by studies in other places with differently selected subjects.

Research on Attitudes

Of the four problems listed above, the study of attitudes has engaged the attention of more investigators over a longer period than any of the others. During the 1920s and 1930s it was a very salient research topic. After World War II, when social psychological research took a marked change of direction, there was for a time a slump in attitude research. Social psychologists were trying to become fully *experimental,* working in laboratories and manipulating the variables. Because it seemed difficult to manipulate attitudes, investigators turned their attention to other problems. But during the 1970s there was a resurgence of interest, and attitudes, like other social variables, were brought into the laboratory. Eagly and Himmelfarb (1978) were able to locate 300 studies they considered important enough to summarize, and they commented on the renewed interest in attitude research. In a later review covering the years from 1977 to 1981, Cialdini, Petty, and Cacioppo (1981) found another 325 studies to report. At present writing, attitude is again a central concept in social psychology.

There were some major accomplishments during the earlier decades. The most conspicuous was the devising of techniques for *measuring* attitudes. Thurstone adapted psychophysical methods that had been used for decades in research on sensation and perception, producing scales along which the attitudes of individuals toward such things as militarism, Prohibition, the church, or a particular race could be measured. Another measuring technique was worked out by Likert, and it too was widely used. Many correlational studies were carried out, relating various attitudes to background variables, personality characteristics, and other things. Probably the most famous of these was the book by Adorno and others (1950), *The Authoritarian Personality*.

There was plenty of evidence for the reliability of attitude scales; they met the standards that had been set for psychological tests. But it was never clear how *valid* they were. Did people actually behave in the ways their scores indicated they would? There was considerable doubt about this until quite recently, when some positive evidence that attitudes are related to behavior began to come in (Ajzen and Fishbein, 1977). What is becoming apparent is that *specific* behaviors are linked to specific attitudes but not to broad attitudes toward a whole category of people or things. For example, Weigel, Vernon, and Tognacci (1974) measured environmental attitudes at different degrees of specificity and later gave students an opportunity to volunteer for Sierra Club activities. The most general measure, the attitude toward a pure environment, correlated only .06 with volunteering, but the most specific, the attitude toward the Sierra Club itself, correlated .68. Fishbein and Ajzen (1975) account for this and similar findings in a model that predicts single acts from *intentions* to act. Intentions are determined by both attitudes and normative pressures. Cialdini, Petty, and Cacioppo (1981) summarize a number of recent studies that demonstrate the importance of level of specificity in attitude and behavior measures as well as other aspects of the total situation in which actions occur, such as commitment, self-awareness, habit, and the opinions of other people.

It is to be noted that, in dealing with this research problem, social psychologists abandoned the single-variable orientation and realized that they must take into consideration multiple variables acting at the same time. They seem not yet to have examined, however, the significance of this change in direction for the "predict and control" objective still accepted as essential for science. In a realm where the same attitude score can reflect different combinations of experience, and the same act can grow out of different tangled roots, is it realistic to suppose that we shall ever be able to predict with any precision just what individuals will do in particular situations? Psychologists try to incorporate more and more variables in the predictive equation, but there are practical limits on the number of aspects of "person in situation" that can be considered simultaneously. Perhaps it is the *objective* that should be changed to allow for a certain amount of unpredictability in the working of every complex system.

Especially during recent decades, most attitude research has been focused on *attitude change*. The principal initiator of this work was Carl Hovland (Hovland, Lumsdaine, and Sheffield, 1949). A behavioral learning theorist, he approached the problem of attitude change by manipulating variables that had been shown to be effective in producing learning of other sorts. In the persuasion experiments that Hovland and his coworkers carried out, the independent variables were classified under three general headings: source, message, and receiver. Here again the multiplicity of factors influencing attitudes became very apparent. In Steiner's table summarizing research on these three types of variables, sixteen separate influences are listed, four under source, eight under message, and four under receiver (1979, p. 541). During the years since Hovland's work, more and more complexity has been encountered. In their review, Cialdini, Petty, and Cacioppo (1981) devote special attention to the receiver end of the sequence. Responses of receivers of persuasive messages range all the way from strong resistance to total acceptance of the attitude being promoted.

One line of research has sought to understand the causes of *polarization* of attitudes. One thing that can happen, especially after group discussion, is that, rather than shifting together to a more negative or positive position, attitudes of individuals in the group become more extreme. Work on this problem extends outside the boundaries of what is usually classified as attitude research and extends to polarization in judgments, preferences, and opinion. Various theories have been proposed about why polarization occurs in some people and situations and not in others, but so far the research has not been definitive.

In general, all the research on how and why attitudes change leads to the same conclusion I have stated before. So many and such diverse variables have been shown to influence the process that it seems unlikely that we will ever be able to "predict and control" it. We need theories and research directed toward some other objective.

One flourishing offshoot of attitude research is the study of person perception, including self-perception. How are one's attitudes toward other persons and oneself developed and changed? Heider (1946) started this ball rolling with the central idea that we try to *balance* our perceptions of other people with our feelings toward them. This is accomplished by liking people who share our views and disliking those who hold opposing ones. For example, if I like Joan and we both strongly disapprove of nuclear power, we can be friends. If I find out that she is in favor of nuclear power, I am not likely to cultivate a relationship with her unless for some reason I change my own attitude on the issue. Countless variations of this basic concept have been used to generate experiments. Over the years, the theory has been partly but not completely supported. Steiner (1979) summarizes major findings by stating that balanced relationships are preferred to unbalanced ones for the people we like but not necessarily for those we dislike. Thus, if I dislike Joan and then find out that we both object to nuclear power, I do not necessarily come to like her any better.

A related research-generating theory was that put forth by Festinger (1957) with *cognitive dissonance* as the central concept. A person strives constantly to maintain balance between acts and attitudes. For example, if a member of a debate team is required to speak in defense of socialism and puts up a strong, persuasive argument, he is likely to find that his own previously procapitalist attitude undergoes modification. Or if, for no identifiable reason, a car buyer decides on a Toyota, her attitudes about other makes of cars and about Japanese imports may undergo gradual change. Research has provided considerable support for the theory, but findings are sometimes ambiguous and can be accounted for in other ways. Here, as in other areas, factors underlying attitude formation and change are complex and involve many variables. The dissonance theory itself has been repeatedly modified to assimilate new research results. It is now recognized that the nature of the decision to carry out the action, such as the debate speech or the Toyota purchase, makes a difference, as do the expected consequences of the action. The requirement that the dissonance-generating act be a free choice among alternatives whose consequences the actor can to some degree foresee is particularly relevant to the central thesis of this book, that any situation provides multiple possibilities and that what a person might have done must be considered if we are to understand what he or she does.

Self-perception theory, especially as formulated by Bem (1972), was for a time viewed as an alternative to dissonance theory. The basic idea was that what causes changes in attitudes to make them conform to previous behavior is simply the person's continual processing of cues on which self-perception, like one's perception of other persons, rests. Each new piece of information one encounters increases the accuracy of one's self-image. Thus, we need not postulate any motivational tension arising from inconsistency. However, we need not consider the cognitive dissonance and self-perception theories incompatible. It is quite reasonable to suppose that some attitude shifts involve dissonance and tension and others do not.

In more recent theorizing about attitudes and the perception of persons, attempts have been made to extend cognitive science, as presented in the preceding chapter, to cover the processing of social information. By assuming that *schemata* for organizing information can be of many sorts, one can apply principles being formulated in cognitive science to schemata of persons, of roles, of events, and perhaps of other entities as well. A symposium volume edited by Higgins, Herman, and Zanna (1981) incorporates a considerable amount of research into this framework. As explained by Taylor and Crocker (1981, pp. 93-94), schemata serve several functions in information processing: They "enable the perceiver to identify stimuli quickly, 'chunk' an appropriate unit, fill in information missing from the stimulus configuration, and select a strategy for obtaining further information, solving a problem, or reaching a goal." Schemata have both representational and interpretive functions. As concrete examples of what social schemata may be like, we might think of Sally's *person* schema of her husband, Bill, incorporating all the information she has accumulated about him, a candidate's *role* schema of hardhat union members that he uses in preparing a speech, and an artist's *event* schema of a promotional cocktail party.

Attribution Research

Much of the thinking and research that social psychologists carried on during the 1960s and 1970s was concerned with the ways people interpret the *causes* of behavior, their own and others'. We are constantly seeking explanations for what individuals do and say to one another. The question asked in so many psychiatrist jokes, "Now just what did he mean by that?," is considered by many psychologists to be the basic social question.

Researchers have been interested in both antecedents and consequences of a person's causal attributions. As Kelley and Michela (1980, p. 460) point out, "Investigators interested in cognitive processes have focused primarily on the antecedents-attributions link and those interested in the dynamics of behavior on the attributions-consequences link." Kelley (1967) presented the first major statement about attribution theory, and the review by Kelley and Michela (1980) provides a summary of what has been accomplished.

The research on antecedents has shown that there are three main factors in a causal attribution. The first is information about what goes with what in the behavior one is trying to interpret. Kelley places a great deal of emphasis on perceived covariation, meaning that an effect is attributed to the factor with which it is seen to covary. For example, if a person uses insulting language only when a friend turns against him and not when an enemy threatens him, the expression of anger is attributed to disappointment or disillusionment rather than to general irritability. The second factor affecting attributions is the beliefs of the person making the causal inference. We can think of these as causal schemata, cognitive structures connecting certain combinations of causes with certain kinds of effects. These have a selective function, so that we consider only some of the alternative meanings of social interchanges. The third factor influencing attributions is the attributor's motivation. This is a complex idea that has stimulated many kinds of research. The first and most obvious question is whether a perceiver is motivated to make any attribution at all. Many of the social interactions we observe every day simply do not matter enough to us so that we think about them at all. However, if there is a high degree of involvement—for example, if our own self-esteem or social standing is at stake—we are predisposed toward some kind of attribution, away from other kinds. Experiments on the effects of motivation for self-enhancement and self-protection have been carried out. Motivation to control situations through one's own efforts has also been studied. The results are far from definitive, although many interesting tentative conclusions have been drawn. Motivation for self-enhancement seems to cause people to attribute success to their own efforts. Motivation for self-protection leads them to attribute failure to situational causes. But because of the interaction of motivation with beliefs and information, these effects do not always appear.

The difficulty psychologists encounter in coming to firm conclusions about causal attributions is compounded by one other factor. Jones and Nisbett (1972) found that it makes a difference whether one is an actor or an observer in a situation. Actors tend to attribute their actions to situational demands. Observers attribute the same actions to stable personality dispositions. As Kelley and Michela point out, this is a finding particularly troublesome for psychologists, because they are always observers in the situations they study. Can they be certain that their attributions about an experiment are any sounder than those made by experimental subjects? The question applies to many other kinds of psychological research besides the kind being discussed here. Psychologists constantly make attributions about the causes of behavior. That is their job. How much confidence can we have in their conclusions?

So far we have been considering research on the antecedents of attributions. Experiments on the consequences for a person of making one attribution rather than another have been difficult and complicated, mainly because there is no generally accepted system for measuring or even classifying attributions, and therefore the independent variable is always somewhat ambiguous. What researchers have done is to locate some sort of distinction that they could make with adequate reliability and then compare groups that differed with regard to this one characteristic. The distinction between extrinsic and intrinsic motivation, for example, has come in for a good deal of study. Extrinsic motivation means that one works to get a reward. Intrinsic motivation means that one works because of interest in the task. An experiment can readily be set up by having one group of subjects engage in an activity they enjoy, and another comparable group get paid for engaging in the same activity. Such experiments tend to show that under reward conditions interest in the activity is reduced. Play is turned into work. However, as with so many research problems, results are not completely unambiguous. The assumption that the attribution the participant makes is "If they have to pay me to do it, it can't be very interesting" may not be sound. There are other ways of accounting for the results.

Another family of experiments designed according to a similar plan compares the attributions made by groups given instructions that lead them to attribute success or failure to skill or to chance. The consequence assessed was the expectation subjects would express of success or failure in the future. Analysis of somewhat confusing results led to the realization that at least two kinds of distinction were involved in the skill/chance comparison. The difference, as subjects see it, may be a matter of stability versus instability. Stable causal factors lead to expectations of continued success; unstable causal factors do not. Or the difference may be a matter of internal versus external control. Attributions to internal causal factors make for pride in success and shame in failure, whereas attributions to external causal factors make for pleasure and displeasure but not pride and shame. Research on locus of control has proliferated in studies of personality, relating this difference to many personality traits as well as social situations (Lefcourt, 1976). Social psychologists have tended to assume that they can produce the attributions they wish to investigate by the instructions they give their subjects at the outset of the experiment. This is not necessarily true, as critics of experimental social psychology have pointed out.

Criticisms of Research in Social Psychology

The foregoing discussions of research on attitudes and on attribution represent only a fraction of what is going on in social psychology. Textbooks of the 1980s have chapters on aggression, prosocial behavior, interpersonal attraction, leadership and power, and a number of other topics. The two topics selected for consideration here can be viewed as illustrative of the approaches being taken to most of the others. What most social psychologists are attempting to do is to set up in the laboratory situations like those they would like to predict and control in the outside world, applying what they consider the basic principles of scientific method as fully as possible. This requires that they formulate hypotheses, select subjects randomly from the population to which they hope to generalize their conclusions, manipulate independent variables both by the instructions and information they give the subjects and by the use of "stooges" (people working with the experimenter, appearing to be subjects but playing roles written into the script). They measure all the variables, independent and dependent.

The recent doubts about these methods that have surfaced in many places are of several kinds. The most cogent criticism has to do with the ethics of manipulation. Is it ever right to deceive people about themselves, to tell them that they have failed when they have actually succeeded, or that they are disliked by their classmates for no understandable reason, or that they are torturing victims by giving them electrical shocks when actually no current is flowing? Investigators have dealt with such ethical criticisms by stressing the debriefing process always carried out at the end of an experiment. Subjects must be fully informed about the purpose of the experiment, the kinds of deception used, and the real facts about their own performance.

But many critics are still not convinced that debriefing wipes out the long-term effects of traumatic experiences in the laboratory. There is also a practical objection to the use of deception in research. More and more people learn not to believe anything a psychologist says. Some psychologists fear that in a few more years the pool of naive subjects whose thinking can be manipulated by instructions will have completely dried up, and social psychology will be bankrupt. Debriefing intensifies this effect by presenting clear evidence that in an experiment things are probably not what they seem.

Another sort of criticism has to do with the generalizability of findings obtained in this way. Reasoning from a hypothesis that is certainly an incomplete statement about some aspects of human nature, the investigator sets up a situation he or she believes to be analogous to one that occurs in the world outside the laboratory. Subjects behave as the hypothesis predicts they will. The investigator draws a conclusion that supports the theory that generated the hypothesis. But often the principle stated in the conclusion does not seem to work in the world outside the laboratory doors, where situations are more complex and contain features psychologists have not noticed before that may influence what people do. The critical question thus becomes: Can we ever create a *usable* social psychology based on laboratory experimentation? Some thinkers advocate field research as a corrective, and there is much more interest in field experiments than there was in previous decades. It is true, as Mook (1983) has pointed out, that generalizability is not important for all experiments. Some are designed simply to test a theoretical hypothesis. But in social psychology, unwarranted generalizations have often been made to the world outside the laboratory.

Another criticism, not so often voiced, has to do with the statistical techniques used to analyze data, techniques that examine general tendencies in groups of subjects but not individual performances. I have mentioned this before in criticizing psychological research in other areas. If, for example, out of fifty subjects who have undergone a failure experience, thirty-five reduce their level of aspiration, whereas only twenty-two out of another fifty who have not been told they failed reduce theirs, and the difference turns out to be "significant at the 5 percent level," the psychologist usually does not even look at what the nontypical subjects in either group did and why. Ways of coping with success, failure, or unfulfilled expectations are numerous and diverse. We need to base our conclusions on the whole range of responses rather than just the average or most frequent one.

Steiner (1979) voices another criticism of research in social psychology. The trouble, as he sees it, is with the basic definition of the subject. A person in a social situation is not just a responder to stimuli. He or she is a stimulator as well, and the sequence of stimuli and responses occurring in even the simplest of social interactions may be an entity with a different structure from the stimuli and responses themselves. What is called into question is the appropriateness of the type of experimental design and analysis that has dominated psychological research in many areas. Some way of studying systems rather than single units of behavior seems to be required. As mentioned earlier, only fairly recently has the growth of general systems theory made this possible.

To sum up what the foregoing criticisms imply, what seems to be needed is a broadened view of what constitutes science. As stated before, "prediction and control" may be the wrong objective. As research proceeded, the number of variables that should be incorporated in prediction equations increased so greatly that accurate prediction of what an individual in a particular situation will do became unworkable, if not impossible. We need to reorganize our science to enable us to think in terms of *sets* of *possible* responses or *repertoires* of *possible* actions rather than single responses to single stimuli. Many proposals are being made for new approaches in social psychology that will meet these criticisms and produce a sounder and more useful body of knowledge about human society. One of these proposed new orientations is a return to action research.

Action Research: An Alternative Direction

During the 1940s and 1950s, while the movement toward rigorous laboratory research in social psychology was taking form, there was quite a different approach that appeared very promising and for a time was very popular. As the years passed, its importance declined almost to the zero point, but with the discontents of the 1970s it came into prominence again. It was called *action research* and was introduced by one of the most creative and charismatic figures psychology has produced, Kurt Lewin. He came to the United States as part of the Hitler outmigration from Germany, where he had been a member of the Gestalt group that was challenging both introspective and behavioristic psychology. Lewin, however, did not simply champion Gestalt principles but proposed bold new theoretical concepts of his own that influenced research in perception, learning, and social psychology. Gestalt psychology had emphasized wholes, whose properties could not be completely analyzed in terms of their parts. Lewin interpreted "wholes" as configurations of forces all acting simultaneously. Each person lived and moved in his or her own "life space" made up of separate areas, with barriers between them and blocked and unblocked pathways connecting them. It was essentially a systems view, put forward long before general systems theory caught the public's attention.

For our purposes here we will ignore Lewin's contributions to the psychology of perception, learning, personality, development, and other major problems and examine his recommendations for research in social psychology. Recognizing that one comes to understand a process as one attempts to change it, and that most effective changes in groups are made by persons who belong to them, he proposed that an investigator actually get into the group being studied, whether as member, discussion leader, or consultant. One can then raise questions, stimulate factfinding and evaluation by group members, and observe a change process while it is occurring (Lewin, 1947). Whether the desired change does or does not occur, the information obtained will enable the researcher to start the process over again with better hope of success. Action research is carried out in groups and proceeds in cycles. The example Lewin cited in the paper just referred to had to do with efforts to bring about wartime changes in food habits. But many other problems have been approached in this way. The group may be made up of students, business executives, or patients on a hospital ward. They must have at the outset some interest in changing something, or at least a sense that something needs to be changed. Action research does not study neutral, value-free psychological processes but, rather, the processes that occur when people are actively trying to improve their situation.

Torbert (1981, p. 437) summarizes the essentials of what he calls "a new model of social science," one that has developed out of action research.

"This new model assumes:
1. That researchers are themselves active participants in the situation researched and that the researcher/situation relationship deserves to be studied.
2. That the framework and variables of studies themselves change in the course of study.
3. That an important way of testing the validity and significance of social knowledge is to feed data back into the setting researched, studying how this feedback influences further action."

The whole volume of papers that includes this chapter by Torbert (Reason and Rowan, 1981) is an attempt to clarify this general research approach. The editors label the approach "New Paradigm Research" because they consider it a radical departure from the model that the social sciences have heretofore been using. In successive sections the authors present the philosophy, the methodology, and some examples of this kind of research. The papers themselves are a mixed bag, and most of the research examples are not particularly impressive, but as a milepost marking a turning point in psychological thinking the book deserves attention. The reader is left with the conclusion that these are indeed the methods of choice for some kinds of social psychological inquiry, although it is difficult to see how they could be applied to all the problems in which psychologists have been interested. At the very least, the formulation of the philosophy and methodology of this different approach gives researchers who are dissatisfied with the predominant one an alternative. As the editors say in the foreword, "What we are contending for in this book is that you don't have to settle for second best. You don't have to accept projects you don't believe in and really don't want to do. You don't have to toe the line of an orthodoxy which is in many ways quite illusory. You can do research which is worthwhile for yourself and for the other people involved in it. You can do research on questions which are genuinely important" (p. xxiii). One might comment, "Spoken in the true spirit of Kurt Lewin, who advocated and tried out this kind of research four decades ago!"

Since Lewin some others have organized their work along lines similar to those he advocated who have often not been thought of as social psychologists. Nevitt Sanford, whose field is generally considered to be personality, is one such person. In a recent paper (1982) entitled "Social Psychology: Its Place in Personology," he connects the two areas. Much of his work has involved interviewing, and his explanation here of what good interviewing is like has much in common with descriptions of action research. Both researcher and researched are involved, and they may both be changed by the experience. The feelings and thoughts of both should be part of the data on which conclusions are based. Sanford cites examples from his own work and from theses done at the Wright Institute. One of these, an intervention at a brewery, in which Foote, as consultant, interviewed department managers, hourly workers, plant managers, and supervisors, individually and in groups, is particularly impressive. The result of this project, to make the plant "a pace-setter for all the nine other plants in the United States in both production and morale," is particularly impressive.

Conclusions

The climate of psychological research is changing, perhaps nowhere more strikingly than in social psychology. Let us summarize the nature of these changes. First of all, it is becoming clear that experimental variables are *multiple* and cannot be completely divorced from one another. This is true for both stimuli and responses. Every stimulating situation has several aspects and can lead to several outcomes. Experimenter and subject *interact*. The experimenter's presence is an aspect of the situation the subject reacts to, and the subject's presence affects the experimenter. Motivational variables generated by the interaction, things like antipathies, prejudices, and positive or negative attitudes, are difficult if not impossible to control.

Second, the statistical techniques used to test hypotheses based on theory are inadequate for research in social psychology because they do not deal with the whole range of responses that individuals and groups make in social situations. The variation here reflects not chance, as assumed in statistical theory, but, rather, alternative adaptive strategies.

Third, recognition of such complications leads to a different kind of theory and a different statement of scientific objective from those most psychologists of the past have espoused. The search for linear cause/effect relationships gives way to the attempt to describe circular system transformations. "Prediction" is superseded by "anticipation"; "control" is superseded by "influence." *Anticipation* and *influence* are terms that leave room for the consideration of multiple possibilities. Manicas and Secord (1983) have presented a new view of what "science" means, one much more compatible with the ideas expressed in this book than the prevailing one is. It would seem to have special relevance to research in social psychology.

CHAPTER 7

Developmental Psychology

❖　❖　❖　❖　❖　❖　❖　❖　❖　❖　❖　❖

Developmental psychology is more difficult to describe than the other research specialties I have discussed. Researchers are of many varieties, work on many sorts of problems, and study many organisms. Three core topics have engaged their attention during the first century of psychology (Cairns and Ornstein, 1979, p. 462):

1. The origins of an activity or pattern of activities.
2. How activities are maintained.
3. How activities are changed in the life history of individual organisms.

At successive periods psychologists have approached these questions from different directions and used different research techniques. Scientists from other disciplines have studied the same problems—zoologists, embryologists, anthropologists, sociologists, and educational researchers. Some have been interested

111

mainly in cognition, others in personality. Some have used animals as subjects, others infants and preschool children, others adolescents and adults of all ages. So far child development has received more attention than either early infancy or adulthood, but this situation is changing in recent decades.

There are four aspects of development that can be differentiated and studied singly or in combination. One can look at biological or social determiners of the developmental process. One can focus on the development of intelligence and other abilities or on the development of motivation and personality characteristics. Each of these main aspects embraces many subaspects. Those who study cognitive development, for example, can focus on the learning of particular *skills* or on the qualitative changes in mental *structure* that occur at successive periods. Some researchers concentrate on the development of language, others on changes in moral standards and behavior. It is obviously impossible to summarize such a diverse body of work in one chapter, but I shall attempt to single out some of the main ideas that have emerged, emphasizing those most relevant to possibility thinking.

A Brief History

Research began about 100 years ago with parents' journal records of individual children. Preyer (1882) carefully observed the day-to-day changes in his son during the first three years of his life, noting when smiling, reaching, sitting up, walking, and talking first occurred and how they changed as time passed. He and the other early journal keepers set standards for careful observation and precise reporting that served as a foundation for all the scientific work that followed.

The decades just before and just after the turn of the century produced two major figures, G. Stanley Hall and James Mark Baldwin. Hall is remembered mainly for the organizing and stimulation he provided for research on development and for his textbook on adolescence (1904). Baldwin (1894) was a brilliant and original theorist, proposing concepts that at the time lacked research substantiation but in recent years have been the focus of much attention.

During the decades between the world wars, most investigators were occupied in collecting factual information about the characteristic behavior of children at successive age levels. Several important child study institutes were organized, and psychologists who worked in them perfected Preyer's observational methods and Hall's questionnaire techniques. Basing their generalizations on samples of children carefully chosen to be as representative as possible, they accumulated normative information about what was to be expected of two-year-olds, five-year-olds, or ten-year-olds, information welcomed eagerly by parents, teachers, and others.

Intelligence testing was a major enterprise of the first half of our century. Some of the early workers were intrigued by the *differences* between individual children of the same age more than by the average or typical performance of age groups. It was Binet who realized that age norms could be used as a measuring device. A child who at two is able to answer questions and solve problems most children cannot handle until they are three is obviously an unusually bright child. And one who at five can just barely succeed at tasks set for four-year-olds can be considered retarded. In his first intelligence scale (Binet and Simon, 1905), Binet simply arranged items in order of difficulty, but in the 1908 revision he proposed that a *mental age* score be assigned according to how far up the ladder an individual child was able to go. He did not take, and probably would not have approved of, the next step, dividing mental age by chronological age to obtain an intelligence quotient (IQ), which has been the source of a great deal of controversy over the years. We need not go into the history of the mental testing movement here but simply note the large part it has played in developmental psychology.

An important offshoot of the work at child development institutes, in which psychologists attempted to plot growth curves for intelligence and many other characteristics, was the initiation of *longitudinal* studies. At first cross-sectional age curves had been plotted by simply connecting the averages for different age groups tested separately. Such curves always showed increases from year to year. In longitudinal studies the same individual children are tested year after year. Curves con-

structed by connecting their successive scores revealed marked
fluctuations. It appeared that the growth of any psychological
characteristic during the childhood years is not a smooth, predictable process. When psychologists turned their attention to
changes during the adult years, the necessity for longitudinal research became even more apparent. If we wish to find out, for
example, whether intelligence declines as people grow older, it
is not enough simply to compare average scores of a group of
twenty-year-olds and a group of seventy-year-olds. Such comparisons invariably show that the young group scores consid-
erably higher than the old. But we must remember that the
whole environment in which today's twenty-year-olds grew up
is so different from the environment for those who were twenty
a half century ago that the groups are not really comparable.
The solution is the longitudinal investigation, in which the same
people are tested at successive ages. During the 1920s and 1930s
several large-scale investigations were initiated, most notably
Terman's study of gifted children and the studies at the University of California and at Fels Institute in which the same subjects were observed from infancy to maturity.

    After World War II, developmental psychology shifted its
emphasis to experiments rather than observations of children.
The preferred approach became laboratory investigation, especially the study of learning, using children as subjects. Much
such research can hardly be called "developmental" at all, as it
does not throw any light on how behavior originates, is maintained, or changes. But it did produce a considerable body of
knowledge that has turned out to have significant practical applications in child rearing, training of the mentally retarded, and
education.

    While most Americans, with their strong preference for
behavioristic approaches, were working along these lines, a new
movement was beginning in Switzerland that was to produce a
profound change in the whole shape of developmental psychology, the work of Jean Piaget. He was both a theoretician and an
empirical researcher, although his research did not follow the
standard experimental model most Americans were using. He
worked with individual children, making detailed observations

of what they did, asking them questions, and performing little informal experiments especially designed to clarify doubtful points. He was not interested in growth curves, test scores, or statistical significance tests. For a while, leading American psychologists ignored him or discounted his work, but by about 1960 that became impossible. From then on, his ideas have dominated developmental psychology throughout the world. Although they have come in for extensive criticism during the 1970s and 1980s, they still provide the theoretical structure on which much of the later theorizing rests.

The essence of Piaget's theory is that child development is not a continuous process but a succession of *stages* that differ qualitatively, not just quantitatively. Furthermore, it is the *constructive activity* of the child adapting to his or her habitat that produces the attainment of the next stage, not just the passive influences of heredity and environment. Piaget differentiated four major stages, each of which was broken down into substages: sensory-motor, from birth to age one and a half or two; preoperational, ages two to five; concrete operations, ages six to twelve; and formal operations, ages twelve and up. At each stage a particular kind of mental structure, or schema, is used in organizing experience, solving problems, and thinking about the world. An example is the early sucking schema, which the infant uses again and again in dealing with objects he or she encounters. As one uses these schemata in more and more situations, they are gradually transformed. The basic processes are *assimilation* and *accommodation.* The organism assimilates when it fits whatever confronts it into an existing schema. An infant, for example, will suck anything her mouth touches, whether it is "suckable" or not. The organism accommodates when it modifies the existing schema to permit the new stimuli to fit into it more easily.

At the first, *sensory-motor* stage, the schemata include physical actions in response to stimulating situations, such as sucking, reaching, or grasping. At the second, *preoperational* stage, schemata involve symbols as well as tangible objects. The child can reach, for example, for a toy he cannot see. The memory image serves as a stimulus. At the third stage, *concrete oper-*

ations, children are able to detach themselves from the real or imagined objects about which they are thinking and perform transformations on their mental images. They can, for example, without changing their own position, report what a scene would look like from different points of view. At the fourth stage, *formal operations,* they deal with symbols of symbols, as it were, entities that have no tangible embodiment, such as truth, honesty, or injustice. At the stage of concrete operations, the child learns to manipulate numbers, but only when the stage of formal operations is attained does manipulation of abstract mathematical concepts become possible. Piagetian theory and the research it has generated will be discussed in more detail later in this chapter.

The 1970s and 1980s have been characterized by the extension of research to hitherto neglected ages, such as early infancy and middle and late adulthood, by attempts to synthesize theoretical concepts initially appearing to be in sharp conflict with one another, and by the general ferment that has stirred up much of psychology. The movement toward cognitive rather than strict behavioristic formulations that has been noted in previous chapters is very evident here. Controversies and conflicts persist, but ways are being found to resolve them. A rapprochement is also occurring between psychologists who are interested mainly in cognition and those interested mainly in personality and motivation. New specialties are being carved out, such as language development, and these are generating theoretical ideas that permeate the whole field.

The Nature/Nurture Issue

The study of human development has deep roots in evolutionary biology. A century ago the word *development* was used to refer to both the evolution of species and the growth changes in individuals. For a long time almost everybody believed that "ontogeny recapitulates phylogeny," meaning that the stages through which the growing organism passes from conception onward are identical with the characteristics of the successive species from which it evolved. Although it is now recognized that this assumption is not strictly true, there is certainly a relationship between species development and individual development.

The question that has given rise to most controversy is the extent to which heredity influences or determines development. Each baby born contains in his or her genes information that will act to initiate all the successive changes in the body—the increases in size, the alterations of proportion of parts to one another, the activation of physiological systems at the proper times. There is ample evidence that information encoded in DNA affects behavior as well as physique. Ethologists have shown how, at a critical time, a duckling, regardless of its previous experience, will start following anything that is moving in front of it. In nature, it follows its mother, but in special circumstances it can follow a different animal entirely or a human being. Birds sing and build nests, beavers construct dams, and leopards pursue prey without having to be taught, although training and practice enable them to perfect the hereditary patterns of behavior. In human animals, pure instinctive behavior of this sort has been harder to identify, but there is little disagreement that to some extent each individual's development is controlled by information in the genes. The question is how decisive such control is.

Research on the "nature/nurture" issue has been continuous over several decades, and interest in it never wanes. Two separate sorts of problem can be differentiated. The first is the question whether the behavioral changes children show as they grow arise mainly from maturation or learning. This problem has been investigated by comparing the progress made over time by comparable children who have been allowed or not allowed to practice a particular skill, such as walking or roller skating. Results have typically demonstrated that children will carry out the activity at about the age it usually shows up whether or not they are trained. Most healthy children, for example, become able to walk even if they have been swaddled tightly or strapped to a board during infancy, as they are in some cultures. But practice also has an effect, and the interaction between maturation and learning has turned out to be far more complex than early investigators thought. What a child is able to do is based on a fusion of hereditary potentialities and experience into schemata that cannot be broken down into hereditary and environmental parts. It is the total organized whole at one stage that is transformed into the pattern of behavior that shows up at the next stage.

The second problem that nature/nurture arguments turn on is the question of differences between individuals and differences between groups. This has been a particularly touchy issue because the widespread use of intelligence tests has continually brought such differences to light. From a theoretical point of view, there is no question that heredity produces individual differences. Each person's chromosomes contain a unique assortment of genes selected randomly from a very large number of possible combinations of the genes of the two parents. Gottesman (1974) has estimated the number of possible genotypes in the world's population at about 70 *trillion*. Consequently, an individual's hereditary developmental potentialities are not identical with those of any other individual, except for identical twins. But there again the interaction between the genetic and environmental determiners is so complex that it is never possible to determine the precise extent to which an individual's intelligence or any other psychological characteristic has been determined by heredity or by environment. At any point in time the organism *is* its total history from conception to the present instant. *"What will be* arises from *what is,* and *what is* is a resultant of the whole history of what has happened when the processes coded in the chromosomes occurred under particular circumstances" (Tyler, 1978a, p. 54).

Scarr and McCartney (1983) are proposing a new theory about the interaction of heredity and environment in development. They contend that the reason the problem has proved so intractable in the past is that investigators have assumed genotype and environment to be *parallel* constructs, whereas they are really qualitatively different and cannot be measured and combined by means of the statistical techniques commonly used. Their central premise is that *"genes drive experience."* Because their genotypes are different, individuals select and interact with different portions or aspects of the total environments to which they are exposed. The theory distinguishes between three kinds of genotype ⟶ environment effects—passive, evocative, and active. As a child grows to maturity, passive influences decline, active influences increase. Increasingly, people choose and to some extent create their own environmental niches, their own habitats.

Learning and Development

Research on learning has played a large part in the thinking that psychologists have done about development. In Chapter Four I have discussed the major directions such research has taken, so that here I will review only the general principles that have been established. One such thread that is woven through the whole fabric of learning research is what has been called the *law of contiguity*. Two experiences, whether of objects, events, or ideas, must be contiguous in space or time if they are to be associated. Philosophers applied this principle to ideas, Pavlov and his successors to unconditioned and conditioned stimuli, Skinner and his followers to acts and their consequences, memory researchers to pairs or lists of nonsense syllables. The second major principle is what Thorndike christened the *law of effect*. In more recent times this requirement for learning has been called *reinforcement*. If an action leads to favorable consequences, whether it be a food pellet for a rat pressing a bar, a word of praise for a schoolchild handing in a paper, or a payment of wages for a job completed, the tendency to repeat the act is strengthened. Endless variations on this theme have been produced as research proceeded. Perhaps the most useful is the distinction between reward and punishment, which have turned out to be not just opposite in their effects but qualitatively different. A third principle that holds for many kinds of learning, but especially for skills of all kinds, is the *law of exercise*, expressed in the adage "Practice makes perfect." There is also a fourth principle less easily embodied in any single word, a principle that has been pointed to again and again, especially since learning researchers turned their attention to language and thinking as well as simpler behavioral responses. What is learned and how well it is learned depend partly on the *meaning* it has for the learner. Stimuli that can be organized into some meaningful pattern are responded to more readily than those that remain fragmentary. What serves as reinforcement for an action depends to a large extent on what the behaving organism *expects.*

Different researchers and theorists have emphasized different ones of these principles. It is possible to bring them all together in describing how skills are acquired, and learned skills are a major factor in development. Research on skill learning has been discussed briefly in Chapter Four. As stated there, recent investigators, such as Anderson (1980) and Fischer (1980), have been focusing attention on cognitive rather than motor skills. Anderson (1980), crediting Fitts and Posner (1967) with the original idea, proposes that the learning of a skill involves three stages: (1) a cognitive stage, in which the learner tries to understand a task, either through his or her own efforts or with the help of a teacher, (2) an associative stage, in which errors in the initial understanding of the task are corrected and separate parts of it are coordinated, and (3) an autonomous stage, in which performance becomes more facile and rapid. Once the autonomous stage is reached, attention need no longer be directed to what one is doing. In fact, attending to the activity may interfere with smooth performance, as athletes and musicians have found out.

To develop as a human being, one must repeatedly go through this learning process to build new skills into the total pattern of one's life. At the beginning, it is others who decide which skills one shall acquire—for example, which language, which code of manners and morals. Increasingly, as one grows, the choice of skills to be cultivated is in one's own hands.

Development as Changes in Mental Organization

A previous section called attention to the importance of the work of Piaget in forcing psychologists to recognize that mental growth is more than the acquisition of responses to stimuli or skills in handling particular situations. Children, even very young ones, *organize* their experience into patterns, or schemata, that they can apply in adapting to the manifold demands life makes on them. People are not just passive recipients of experience, passive responders to stimuli. They interpret situations, constantly trying to make sense of their worlds. Piaget was as much philosopher as psychologist, and his major focus was on this constructive process. He called his system *genetic epistemology*. It was the changes in the shape of the mental structures through which individuals screen experience that mainly interested him. The stages and substages he analyzed describe the organization of these successive structures. He was not content to conclude, as many unsophisticated intelligence testers do, simply that the child thinks "better" or "more correctly" as he or she grows older. The important thing for Piaget is that the child thinks *differently*.

One kind of experiment came to have a special significance in the research Piaget and his followers did, research on *conservation*. It took many forms. One was to present a child with two identical tall, thin containers of water and then to pour the water from one of them into a short, wide container, asking the child whether the amount of water in the newly filled container was more than, less than, or the same as the amount in the other tall, thin one. If the subject is at the preoperational stage, the answer is likely to be that the new glass has more because it is wider or less because it is shorter. It is not until a child reaches the stage of concrete operations that it becomes obvious that the amount of water does not change when poured from one container into another. The young child does not *conserve* volume. Conservation of quantity is one of the earmarks of the concrete operational stage. Several kinds of conservation have been explored experimentally. Conservation of length can be tested by confronting the subject with two identical rods side by side and then moving one of them forward or backward a little and asking whether they are the same length. Conservation of number is studied by moving marbles from one pile to another, conservation of weight by still other maneuvers.

Out of these and other Piagetian experiments, one serious challenge to the whole theory of stages has arisen. It is the problem of *decalage,* or unevenness. A child may pass the water container test with flying colors but be unable to demonstrate conservation of weight or number. Has he reached the stage of concrete operations or not? Difficulties of this sort have led some psychologists to discard the whole concept of mental stages in favor of theories that children do only the specific things they have learned to do. Others, such as Flavell (1982), are attempting to enlarge and modify Piagetian theory to fit the research findings. Flavell analyzes the possible sources of both heterogeneity and homogeneity at a given stage, showing that both are to be expected. Some strands of development remain quite independent of others, even when most strands are woven into the kind of network Piaget postulates. Psychologists who give individual intelligence tests have recognized this fact for years. Five-year-old Peter, for example, may pass the diamond drawing test at the seven-year level even though he is unable to succeed with any of the tests for six-year-olds. Either the growing individual's unique assortment of genes or unique environment may tend to make him or her better at some specific tasks involving some specific kinds of material than at others calling for the same thinking process. A child high in mechanical aptitude but low in verbal aptitude will be able to put the parts of a puzzle together more successfully than she can put words together.

Flavell holds that unevenness traceable to these sources does not mean that the Piagetian concept of qualitatively different stages is wrong or useless, because along with the factors making for heterogeneity there are other factors making for homogeneity. It is not an all-or-none matter. To characterize a child as having reached the stage of concrete operations still has meaning, especially for tasks that have been thoroughly mastered and well practiced. Such tasks will all be performed with about the same level of expertness. The heterogeneity appears when harder and less familiar problems are presented. With still harder tasks, performances are homogeneous again—consistent failure. Such results are exactly what individual intelligence testing, using a Binet-type scale, has shown. Susy, for example, passes all the tests for ten-year-olds, half of those for eleven-year-olds, a few of those for twelve-year-olds, and none at any higher level.

Fischer (1980) has proposed a theory that puts together all these ideas, with a place for both Piaget's qualitatively different stages and Skinner's separately learned specific behaviors. Fischer prefers the term *levels* to *stages* for the successive steps on the developmental ladder, differentiating ten of these in all. Each level is transformed into the next by the learning of skills, sets of skills, and sets of sets of skills. The theory, though complex, promises to resolve some of the major conflicts that have arisen in theorizing about cognitive development. Paris and Lindauer (1982), approaching the problem from the same neo-Piagetian point of view, emphasize the importance of what they call *metacognition* in the transformation process that moves the child from level to level. This has to do with the thinking one does about thinking, the evaluation of one's own abilities and mental states, the selection of strategies to meet task goals, and the monitoring and regulating of progress. Each person is to some extent the architect of his or her own development. Metacognition is becoming an increasingly popular topic for research.

Building on the foundation Piaget laid, the key concepts of assimilation and accommodation are also being reexamined and clarified. Block (1982, p. 286) proposes to revise Piaget's assumption that the two processes occur simultaneously or almost simultaneously in every adaptive act and thinks of them instead as *alternative strategies.*

> I suggest, in a more explicit and stronger form than can be found in Piaget's writings, that through the course of evolution, individuals have been programmed to follow the adaptive imperative: "Assimilate if you can, accommodate if you must." Assimilatory efforts are the first line of adaptation. When assimilation works or can be made to work, it is adaptively economic, preserving

existing equilibrations of cognitive structures and maintaining the individual in a tolerable or sufficient state. It is only when assimilation fails, for whatever reason, to reconcile intrusions within the structural status quo that the destructured individual attempts the second line of adaptation, accommodation. Whereupon the formation of new structures, if effective, can be used to assimilate, thus again equilibrating the individual. As Piaget emphasized many times, the repeated interplay of these meaning-making strategies provides a heuristic for adaptation of profoundly wide and profoundly deep applicability.

Block goes on to discuss the applicability of these ideas to the domain of personality as well as cognition, with which Piaget has been mainly concerned, showing how they account for the many sorts of differences between individuals that we observe, as well as for the general course of social and emotional growth.

Social-Emotional Development

Since the beginning of our century, alongside the stream of research on intelligence and other cognitive characteristics has been a parallel stream of thinking about social-emotional-motivational development. A convenient starting point for the consideration of this psychological question, as for so many others, is what Freud had to say about it. Although his thoughts about development were at first stimulated by and applied to only the neurotic adults he was trying to help, they soon spread to the interpretation of the lives of normal people as well and supplied a framework within which observational studies of children could be conducted.

Psychoanalytic therapy involves digging back into early memories for the roots of the patient's disorders. It is a basic tenet of psychoanalysis that much motivation is unconscious and that painful memories are especially likely to have been repressed. For this reason, it is never easy to uncover memories of crucial childhood experiences. Freud assumed that an individual possessed from birth a supply of psychic energy that was discharged and channeled differently as development proceeded. He considered this energy to be basically sexual in nature, even at early ages before the beginning of obvious sexual behavior. Like Piaget, he differentiated stages, but they were stages in psychosexual direction rather than cognitive organization. The first is the *oral* stage, when satisfaction comes mainly through mouth activities, sucking and later biting. It lasts from birth to about one year of age. The second is the *anal* stage, from about one to three years of age, when satisfaction is derived from expelling or withholding urine and feces. The third is the *phallic* stage, from about three to five years of age, when satisfaction is obtained by stimulation of the genital organs. Toward the end of this period, the *Oedipus complex* is the dominant feature of development. The child has incestuous feelings for the parent of the other sex (the concept was never as clear for girls as for boys) and finally resolves the conflict they produce by identifying with the rival parent. This may take some time, and from about age six through twelve there is a *latency* period, when sexual feelings are repressed and friendships with peers of the same sex become the principal sources of satisfaction. With puberty the *genital* stage begins, which lasts for the rest of life. Relationships with members of the other sex increasingly become the way psychic energy, or *libido,* is discharged and satisfaction obtained. This brief summary is obviously an oversimplification of a very complex process. Volumes have been written about it. Individual variations on the basic themes are endless. Many of the difficulties Freud's patients (and those of later therapists) complained of could be viewed as *fixations* at a particular developmental stage or *regressions* to an earlier stage.

Building on the foundation Freud had laid, Erikson (1963) proposed a stage theory that incorporated social influences as well as instincts. His theory was extended to the adult years as well as childhood. The core idea is that the growing individual, in adapting to his or her world, especially the world of other people, is faced with successive challenges or motivational conflicts to be resolved. Briefly, the Eriksonian stages, labeled according to these challenges, are as follows:

1. Basic trust versus mistrust—first year of life.
2. Autonomy versus shame and doubt—ages one to three.
3. Initiative versus guilt—ages three to six.
4. Industry versus inferiority—ages six to twelve.
5. Identity versus role confusion—adolescence.
6. Intimacy versus isolation—late adolescence and early adulthood.
7. Generativity versus stagnation—middle adulthood.
8. Ego integrity versus despair—late adulthood and old age.

The ages specified are, of course, only approximate. The first five stages cover the same childhood period as Freud's stages; the last three are additions to the Freudian list to cover the rest of life. Each stage is a whole system of concepts about the self in relation to others; each involves decisions and choices. Problems not solved or unsatisfactorily solved in one period persist into later ones.

Stage theories have stimulated research in many special areas, most notably Kohlberg's work on stages in moral development (Kohlberg, 1976). With or without stage concepts, psychologists have investigated many aspects of the development of personality, including attachment, aggression, sex-typing, affective processes, and psychopathology. Some have explored changing relationships of child to family, others changing relationships to peer groups. Development during the adult years is a flourishing field of research (Baltes, Reese, and Lipsitt, 1980).

There have been some attempts to generate theories that would bring together cognitive and noncognitive development—linking Freud and Piaget, as it were. Chandler and Boyes (1982), for example, explain social and moral development in Piagetian terms. The social cognition underlying social relationships they see as essentially *role taking,* and this process changes qualitatively as the child grows. A person is able to assimilate only knowledge at or below his or her own level and thus is limited in the capacity to understand other people. No amount of reasoning or exhortation can enable a preoperational child to take the role of a mature parent or older sibling. He or she is bound to misrepresent or misconstrue it. Much misunderstanding could be avoided if this were recognized by caretakers of young children.

General Features of the Emerging Synthesis

As the number of subareas in developmental psychology has increased and psychologists have focused their research efforts on narrower and narrower specialties, it has seemed to many that the days of comprehensive theories like Piaget's or Erikson's are over. However, certain general features of all or most of the research make it appear possible, at least, that someone will eventually offer a satisfactory synthesis.

The first of these features characterizing present thinking is one I have discussed at length in previous chapters, the shift to general systems theory. This orientation is particularly appropriate to the study of development. A human being at any stage is a system in which every part is linked to every other part in an organized way. Systems are always in the process of transformation. Each change in a part affects the shape of the whole. A one-year-old who has just learned to walk is not just the same baby plus a new skill. He is a different creature who can be expected to function differently in a number of ways. An individual's intelligence cannot be described as a fixed amount of hereditary capacity plus the extensions that an enriched environment has added. It is a system of thinking whose organization incorporates all the adaptations to many different situations that the person has made so far.

Another salient feature of recent work is the emphasis on *reciprocity*. It is recognized that while a child is responding to stimulation provided by the mother, the mother is responding to stimulation provided by the child. The two psychological systems are being transformed at the same time, and a system constituted by the interaction between them is being created and re-created. Both positive and negative feedback are constantly transforming the systems. Reciprocity makes the task of

observing children in their environments very complex, but they
are observable. Parents and teachers are becoming aware of the
ways children are shaping them as they attempt to shape the
children.

Another concept discussed in previous sections has come
to occupy a prominent place in research and theories about development, the *schema,* or mental structure through which information is processed and action controlled. Children do not
just react passively to the situations and information they encounter. They categorize and organize, and then apply the resulting schemata in adapting to new situations, processing new
information. And the schemata that individuals use are incredibly numerous and diverse.

Another concept being widely used in discussions of development is *strategy,* meaning a general plan for dealing with
adaptational challenges. Strategies may come into existence
spontaneously or be deliberately thought out. The extent to
which performance can be improved by deliberately teaching
appropriate strategies is of considerable interest, both theoreti-
cally and practically.

As mentioned earlier in the chapter, the concept of *metacognition* seems increasingly important, the child's own awareness of the schemata used in processing information and the
strategies used in meeting new situations. Each experience develops and enriches one's concept of the *self.* Bandura (1982a)
is one of the theorists who place much emphasis on the part
that self-understanding plays in development. One's assessment
of *self-efficacy* enters into every learning situation—cognitive,
behavioral, emotional, or social. If a child does not see himself
as able to carry out an assigned task, no promised reward is likely to induce him to try it. Just telling a child "You can do it"
has very little effect, as generations of parents and teachers have
discovered.

The concepts most closely related to the theme of this
book are those having to do with possibilities, alternatives, and
choices. As in other research fields, the trend over time has been
from simplicity to complexity, from single variables to multiple,
interacting variables, from the passive organism to the active,

autonomous self, from a search for factors *determining* out-comes to a search for factors *influencing* them. Perhaps more clearly in developmental research than in research on other problems, psychologists have given up the fruitless quest for complete predictability. In any observable circumstances there is always more than one possible outcome. Not all children of schizophrenic parents become psychotic; not all low-IQ nursery school children turn out to be retarded; not all abused children end up as abusers of their own children. And conversely, not all well-adjusted teenagers grow into mature, competent adults. The answer to the question "How will this person turn out?" is always "It depends." The multiplicity of factors influencing de-velopment makes for a modicum of uncertainty; but it also engenders hope. Because there is more than one possibility, and because the human animal is capable of choice, our futures are at least partly in our own hands.

PART III

What the Concept
of Multiple Possibilities
Means to Individual Lives

❖ ❖ ❖ ❖ ❖ ❖ ❖ ❖ ❖ ❖ ❖ ❖

The concept of multiple possibilities has implications not only for the production of psychological knowledge, research, and its products but also for the utilization of such knowledge. In pursuing a psychological career, there have always been two main directions a person might take. The first is the research path, discussed in some detail in the preceding chapters. The other is the professional path, which requires that one apply the knowledge one has acquired in the service of humanity. The World 3 habitats of the two kinds of psychologist are different in many respects—the university or research institute for the "pure" scientist, the clinic, school, consulting office, or industrial organization for the "applied" scientist. Their associates, the books they read, the meetings they go to, and the things they worry about will all be different.

The two habitats do, however, overlap to a considerable extent. All psychologists hold some common values. Ideally they should all be adding to our store of usable knowledge and

131

should all contribute to human welfare. Conflicts over the use of psychological resources inevitably occur, but over the years there has been general agreement that it is an advantage to keep the two enterprises, knowledge production and knowledge utilization, in contact with each other.

The changes discussed in Part One in basic assumptions about what constitutes science are particularly helpful for professional or practicing psychologists. Rigidly deterministic assumptions impede therapeutic and educational efforts. For example, if it were true that personality defects in adults inevitably followed from unfavorable conditions during the first year of life, the prospect for their elimination in a few hours, or even a few years, of therapy would not be bright. Furthermore, multiple possibilities are very evident in the conduct of therapy itself. There is no one right way to proceed with helping. There was a time when child training manuals specified exactly what parents should and should not do. Such manuals have become scarce in recent years. We know that there are many paths to normal development and that outstanding adults have undergone many different kinds of treatment as children. There was a time when psychoanalysis was almost the only treatment for personality disturbances. By now a person seeking help can choose from dozens of approaches to therapy. There was a time when human nature was thought to be the same the world over. We now recognize the multiplicity and diversity of human nature. Cultural, national, and individual differences are not only recognized but valued. The psychologist intervening in a person's life tries to help the client to see and develop unique possibilities for a rewarding life rather than to think and behave like a "normal" person.

The utilization of psychological knowledge involves more than just the activities of professional psychologists. It is a matter of presenting the knowledge directly to the public to be used in the conduct of their own lives. Some years ago (1969) George Miller, in a presidential address to the American Psychological Association, proposed that a part of the responsibility of each of us is to "give psychology away." The statement has been widely quoted and very influential. More and more public schools are adding psychology courses to their curriculum. Newspaper stories and magazine articles have been increasing in number and improving in quality. Through popular books, television, and radio, psychological knowledge is being presented to the public. Individual psychologists, whatever their specialties, make their expertise available by means of lectures and consultation. This section of the book will explore the relevance of the concept of multiple possibilities to some of these efforts.

CHAPTER 8

Bringing Up Children

❖ ❖ ❖ ❖ ❖ ❖ ❖ ❖ ❖ ❖ ❖ ❖

Perhaps the most valuable contribution psychology can make to our society is to improve the rearing of children. It has often been pointed out that the human species is unique in the length of time it takes to produce a mature individual. As pet owners know, a puppy in less than a year grows into a dog capable of carrying out a dog's full responsibilities. Most birds leave the nest and learn to fly within a few weeks of hatching and are soon ready for the long migrations they must undertake. In contrast, human children require a long growing period, during which time many sorts of influences help to determine what kind of adults they will be.

In an earlier chapter I have discussed the complexity of the interaction between the program written in one's genes and environmental influences. Almost all human children learn to walk, but the time it takes to acquire the skill, one's characteristic gait, and a positive or negative attitude toward walking, compared with riding or being carried, vary with the circumstances.

It is natural for a child to talk, even to talk grammatically, but both the speed with which one develops the ability and the level of proficiency eventually attained depend on what the adult caretakers do. More complex and difficult skills like bicycle riding, violin playing, ballet dancing, or driving a car never develop at all unless the right environmental opportunities are present. Talents or aptitudes for athletic or musical performance are carried in the genes, but the skills themselves must be learned. The point is that in emphasizing the importance of childrearing I am not discounting the importance of heredity. Nature equips the person with multiple possibilities for development; nurture determines which ones will be developed and how well they will be actualized.

What, in general, is a desirable habitat for a growing child? In the first place, there are certain basic needs that must be met. It is obvious that from the beginning one must have food and warmth and physical care. It is clear, however, that there are more possible ways of meeting these needs than people used to assume there were. Another basic need that a growing body of research findings is pointing out is *attachment* to some caring adult. Ordinarily this person is the mother, but it can be another person who is always there, always available, like the "nanny" in a wealthy English family or one special nurse in a hospital or orphanage. It is the failure to meet this need that has been shown to retard the development of many institutionalized children, children who are fed, dressed, and exercised by hired workers who may be kind enough but have no interest in individual children. This research fits well into Erikson's formulation of the challenge a child faces during the first year of life, to acquire a solid conviction that people can be trusted. It is not impossible to overcome basic mistrust at later developmental stages, but the child who learns trust early is better prepared for all the later challenges (see the next section for fuller discussion).

Another need is for an opportunity to learn essential skills that everybody in one's cultural group practices. From toilet training to table manners to finding one's way around the neighborhood, it is important that explicit training be available. In our culture reading and writing are considered essential for everybody; in others swimming or target shooting may be required of all. The more expeditiously one can learn these behavior patterns, the faster and smoother one's progress up the developmental slope will be.

The next need is for cognitive input. This means not just giving out all sorts of information but setting up conditions favorable to the formation of cognitive structures to use in organizing it. It is natural for children to form categories for classifying the facts, people, and experiences they meet in their dealings with the world, but how correct and inclusive the categories are depends a great deal on the help they get from adults. For example, all children by a certain age use a male/female category, but the meanings they attach to the distinction as applied to play, work, and appropriate behavior vary widely, and some meanings are much better adapted than others to the world they must face. Adults can help children correct and refine their category systems.

One other need, closely related to the central theme of this book, is for facilitation of choices and commitments. Inevitably one grows into only one of the persons one might have been, but whether developmental direction is shaped by haphazard influences or by personal decisions makes a difference in how one sees oneself. Here again, Erikson's theory is pertinent. The challenge of adolescence, as Erikson views it, is identity versus role confusion. Making choices about which of one's possibilities one will build on leads to a firm sense of personal identity and a feeling of being in control of one's life.

Responsibilities of Parents and Parent Surrogates

It is usually parents who are responsible for giving children the right start in life. However, as society has grown more complex, and families and social agencies have become more diversified, it is becoming clear that others can take on some or all of the responsibility for meeting children's needs without ill effects on the children. When I talk about the mother's responsibility for the care of young infants, for example, I mean that there must be some mothering person to play this role. Older siblings of young children often take it on. Foster mothers play it well. Even in institutions like hospitals and orphanages, a nurse or aide can become a "mother" to a particular child. As rigid sex roles are being relaxed in our time, we find that some fathers handle the "mothering" of young children very adequately.

Before discussing in any detail how the basic needs of children are met during the early years, I should say something about the much-researched question of just how important *early* experience is in the total developmental process. Only a few decades ago, it was being suggested that the first few years were *all*-important for normal intellectual and emotional development and that failure to undergo certain crucial experiences at critical periods must necessarily handicap a person for life. A pioneer in this line of research was Spitz (1945), who showed that babies placed in institutions where they received impersonal care developed a psychological condition he called "anaclitic depression," characterized by weeping, apathy, and withdrawal. Other investigations of both children and animals indicated that failure to receive the necessary stimulation at the proper time interfered with intellectual growth. Goldfarb (1943, 1944) carried the research one step further in a follow-up study that revealed striking differences in intellectual, social, and emotional characteristics between a group of adolescents who had spent their first three years in institutions and another group who had spent them in foster homes. The foster-home group was clearly superior.

Since the time of these studies new evidence has been presented that handicaps arising from early deprivation can be overcome. Not everybody raised in an orphanage suffers from anaclitic depression. Some children from poor, nonstimulating homes and neighborhoods become highly intelligent adults. Heredity, of course, may play a part in the differences between individuals, as has been explained before. The genes a person is endowed with may happen to be more favorable for development than those of his or her parents or siblings. But present writers also emphasize the *plasticity* of the human organism during the whole course of development (Cairns, 1979). Early experience is important for intellectual, social, and emotional growth, but so is later experience. J. McV. Hunt, who has made some of the most important contributions to this body of knowledge, sums up the matter this way: "In human beings the preschool years, and especially the first three of them, appear to be highly important for the achievement of initiative . . . , of trust . . . , of compassion, . . . and of curiosity, and of various still poorly understood attainments . . . that seem to be important for the later development of competencies. Yet plasticity can cut both ways. A major share of early losses can be made up if the development-fostering quality of experience improves, and a great deal of early gain can be lost if the quality of experience deteriorates" (1979, p. 136).

With these caveats in mind, we can still say that the progress of research has borne out Erikson's statement that the first need of the child is to develop basic trust, a trust that arises most readily from the experience of loving care by someone one is close to. On the foundation of emotional security rest all the kinds of learning that make life rich and complete. What we now realize is that mothering during infancy is not the only possibility for the building of this foundation, and it can be built later than the first few months of life. A fortunate child is secure in the love of parents from the beginning, but a child who has suffered from several years of orphanage care may make rapid progress once adopted into a loving home. Even as an adult, a person whose psychological development has been warped by the lack of basic trust may acquire it in a relationship with a trusted therapist. What is important is for this need to be met as early as possible in life. The first imperative for not only parents but also daycare center workers, kindergarten teachers, mental health workers, and many others who deal with children is to treat each individual in such a way that security and trust result from the relationship. The adult's attitude must be genuine; it cannot be faked.

This is not always so easy as it may appear. Some children are much easier than others to love. Some babies are cute and cuddly; others are not. Some preschoolers are friendly and sociable, others standoffish or hostile to strangers. One salient fact that has emerged from recent research is that relationships are reciprocal; they work both ways. What parents do affects children's feelings and behavior, but at the same time, what the children are doing affects the feelings and behavior of the parents. Child abuse, an urgent social problem of our time, is often understandable in these terms. However it got started in the first place, continued whining and crying in a two-year-old is very irritating to her father, who wants to settle down in peace to watch a game on TV. He speaks sharply to the child, who as a result whines and cries even more. Both father and child get more and more miserable until, on an impulse, the father knocks the child against the wall when she comes near, swinging harder than he meant to. The child is knocked unconscious, the mother rushes her to the hospital, the doctor notifies the police.

General systems theory, discussed in early chapters, has been useful in thinking about situations like this. Research is now going on using as units dyads or triads or even whole families rather than individuals, and therapy is being designed to change the way the system is working rather than to change the participants separately. Sometimes a parent who senses the growth of a negative attitude toward a child can analyze the interactive system, but often it is helpful to have a skilled professional take a look at it. In the case of the father and child described above, the mother or a clinical psychologist who has been called in might be able to see that a change in Sally's schedule could head off the whining spell, a change such as feeding her earlier than the rest of the family and sending her out for an evening play period. Or perhaps the TV set could be moved to a room where the door could be closed, and Sally's whining ignored by the rest of the family. It is characteristic of system modification that there are alternative possibilities. Thus, if one does not work, something else can be tried. One thing that is clear from research and clinical practice is that it is important to recognize and acknowledge troublesome attitudes, not just attempt to mask or deny them.

One trend that seems especially promising is the increasing availability of self-help groups that make it possible for parents to support and assist one another. In one city, for example, there is an organization called Birth-to-Three, with membership open to all parents of children in this age group. (Parents are not just *allowed* to belong; they are sought out and welcomed. For each birth the newspaper of the city lists, an invitation to join is sent to the new mother.) Joining makes parents participants in neighborhood groups where common concerns are discussed. Other services are also provided, not the least of which is a monthly newsletter providing expert information about special problems. A recent issue, for example, explains everything parents might want to know about how to travel with a small child. The newsletter also lists coming events, such as lectures and workshops, that might interest some of the readers.

The next need I listed is for training in essential skills. This is not altogether independent of the need for emotional security. Because of the reciprocity factor, failure to meet a training need may render a child very difficult for parents or anyone else to live with. Helping parents with efficient techniques of toilet training, for example, therefore also helps them to maintain the right relationship and home atmosphere.

The technology based on behavior modification, discussed in some detail in an earlier chapter, is especially useful in such skill training. The steps to be followed are simple:

1. Analyze exactly what it is you want the child to do, if necessary breaking the action down into simpler components to be trained separately.
2. Design a situation in which the act will occur. Sometimes this can be done by *modeling*. At other times the process of successive approximations that Skinner called *shaping* can be initiated.
3. Reinforce the behavior by an immediate reward until it occurs regularly even without reinforcement.
4. Be careful not to reinforce any undesirable behavior that occurs in the same situation.

Notice that the simple absence of reinforcement, rather than punishment, is recommended to get rid of unwanted behavior. Punishment is not really the opposite of reward. Its effects are complex. Even when it leads to a cessation of undesirable behavior, it still may give the child no clue about what he or she should have done instead. There are many possible things a child may do when induced by punishment to stop doing one particular thing. Some of these may be worse than the behavior the parent was trying to eliminate. The consequences of reward are predictable; the consequences of punishment are not. Furthermore, punishment often produces undesirable emotional consequences. If the thrashings Sally receives make her hate and fear her father for the rest of her life and rebel against all authority, she has paid too high a price for whatever good they may initially have done.

However, some kinds of bad behavior must be stopped. The concept that has replaced punishment is the concept of *limits,* applied when children are endangering themselves or others or behaving in ways that are obnoxious to parents and associates. There are various ways to impose limits. The simplest, especially with very young children, is restraint, holding the child in such a way as to prevent an undesirable action from occurring. It is a natural response to the sight of a child heading for an open fire or wading into deep water. After the child has learned to understand language, limits can be set up verbally. "You must *never* run into the street, no matter what happens!" One technique widely used by behavior modifiers is called "time out." A screaming child may be confined in an empty room where there is nothing to damage and very little stimulation of any kind until the mood passes. A child making a mess with the food on his plate instead of eating can be removed to the bathroom and left there with the door closed for a short time.

Although the steps just outlined are simple to conceptualize, they are often very difficult to put into practice. Designing a special training situation for a particular child requires a high degree of ingenuity. Children differ in many ways—understanding of verbal instructions, tendency to follow a model, and susceptibility to different kinds of reinforcement. Self-help groups are often useful here. What one mother has found works may be exactly what another mother needs to try. Ingenuity is a salient characteristic of the psychologists who specialize in applications of behavior modification, so that through consultation parents may get ideas that would never have occurred to them without it. The psychologist can often suggest some change in an overall situation that will make the system function differently. For example, in one instance a mother found herself becoming more and more angry and impatient with her eight-year-old son, who never came directly home from school but wandered away and often got into trouble. What she failed to see, but what a psychologist quickly spotted, was that the increasingly severe scoldings she was administering when he did get home were exacerbating the problem. The solution was to devise some means to induce him to come home directly at least once and then reward him when he got there. Perhaps driving to the school and picking him up would work, or perhaps an older neighbor child could watch for him and walk home with him. Then greeting him with a smile and a snack or even taking him to the zoo might work as reinforcement. There are, of course, many other possibilities. Together the mother and the psychologist worked out a plan. A few days of the new procedure was enough to instill the new habit.

It is quite apparent that wise parents, teachers, and animal trainers have been applying for years the principles recommended here, long before Skinner or anyone else enunciated them or produced scientific evidence for their validity. In many, perhaps most, families such intuitive wisdom is all that is needed, and advice from psychologists is at best distracting, at worst harmful. But teaching people techniques of behavior modification has at least two purposes. For one thing, it is a way of dealing with stubborn malfunctions that sometimes appear in the course of development even when all has been well up to that time. Another, related benefit is that knowledge of these principles makes it possible for people who rear children to analyze what they are doing and trying to do and to locate flaws in the designs they are using.

People tend to be much more punitive than they think they are. The assumption that the best way to control behavior is through punishment has very deep roots in our society, surfacing in a wide variety of institutions, such as schools, legal procedures, laws, and penal institutions. Unthinkingly we often take it for granted that the way to instill good behavior is to punish bad behavior. There may be a kernel of soundness in this attitude. In a totalitarian society, it would be possible ideally to train all citizens in all the right habits by punishing wrong behavior and thus produce a smoothly functioning system. Skinner's novel *Walden Two* depicts such a society. But in a society where personal freedom is a central value, the ideal is to rule out rather than to punish behavior that is completely unacceptable but to leave individuals free to choose what they will do instead. The fact mentioned before, that punishment does not convey as much information as reward, may thus be its major advantage in a free society. It is *limits* rather than punishment that the system requires, and there are many ways of setting and enforcing them. To discuss fully the social implications of this idea would carry us far away from the topic of this chapter, so I will not pursue the subject here.

So far I have been talking about the building of skills or habits. Skills that all children must acquire, such as appropriate bladder and bowel control, can be developed in this way. So can the special skills that only some children have the wish and the opportunity to acquire, such as piano playing, dancing, or horseback riding. Academic skills and occupational skills are in the same category. But adding skill to skill, habit to habit, is not all there is to development. Another objective is what I like to call the "well-stocked mind." A human being's mental equipment is not just a well-oiled, functioning machine but a storehouse of information.

It is apparent, especially after the development of language, that it is natural for children to reach out after information about many things. (The development of language itself, a topic of much interest to current researchers, is partly a matter of skill, partly a matter of information.) What has not been so generally recognized until research on cognitive psychology brought it to the forefront of attention is that the storing, retrieval, and utilization of information involve *organization* and that the mental structures children develop to organize information are important to understand. In Chapter Four I used the word *schema* as a label for the mental structures used to organize information. Different theorists have used the term with slightly different meanings. I use it broadly to cover all or most of the things they have meant by it. A good definition is the one by Taylor and Crocker (1981, pp. 93–94), quoted in a previous chapter: Schemata "enable the perceiver to identify stimuli quickly, 'chunk' an appropriate unit, fill in information missing from the stimulus configuration, and select a strategy for obtaining further information, solving a problem, or reaching a goal." Information to be stored must be organized, and each of us develops a unique assortment of pigeonholes.

Thus, the third responsibility of people who rear children is to create situations that will facilitate the formation of useful schemata and the storage of as much useful information as possible. Piaget's principles of assimilation and accommodation, discussed in the preceding chapter, are applicable here. A child attempts to fit new information into existing schemata. This enlargement necessitates modification of these schemata. Schemata cannot be given to a child; one must grow them for oneself. What the adult caretaker can do is, first of all, to listen and watch in order to become aware of the schemata now operative. If they seem inadequate, as, for example, when racial or sexual stereotypes are in evidence, the child can be confronted with situations that make it necessary to enlarge and modify them. This, of course, is likely to happen naturally as the child's world broadens. For example, one little girl, addicted to fairy tales, classified people into the beautiful and the unbeautiful. All through second grade, she tolerated her unbeautiful teacher, hoping to be transferred into the other second-grade classroom, where the beautiful teacher was. Finally a transfer was arranged, but alas, the little girl found that Miss Sweeney, the beautiful teacher, was irritable and unloving, given to sharp reprimands, reluctant to answer questions or help with assignments. The contrast between the two teachers led to a modification of the schema. The new classification was "good" versus "not good."

The other thing caretakers can do is to feed the child's hunger for information of all sorts. Conscientious parents have always sensed the importance of answering children's questions about all sorts of things—the stars, African animals, where babies come from, and innumerable others. Conscientious teachers have also taken seriously their obligation to convey information, but they sometimes think of it as something to be pumped into a child's mind like water into a tank, rather than as material for the child to organize. The acquisition of organized information is not just the learning of facts. Many sorts of experience promote the processes of assimilation and accommodation, experiences such as summer camp, part-time jobs, and travel to far places. Each problem or challenge the child meets leaves its residue. Hunt (1961) has emphasized again and again what he calls "the problem of the match." The challenge must not involve a schema too similar to or too different from the one the child habitually uses. If it is too similar, lack of progress and boredom result; if it is too different, there is also lack of progress, accompanied by frustration, withdrawal, and a diminished sense of self-efficacy. Bullock (1981, p. 104) expresses the same thought in the succinct statement that "people characteristically steer themselves between the two negative poles of cognitive overload and boredom." Arranging for this match in real-life situations is an *art* that too few child caretakers have mastered.

Recent research (Higgins, Herman, and Zanna, 1981) has shown that social information, like other information, involves the formation and modification of schemata. Children classify the people they come to know into categories and relate new social experience to these, as the example of the little girl and the beautiful teacher illustrates. The categories tend to be overly broad or overly narrow to start with, such as Americans, Italians, Finns, family members versus all others, or adults versus children. They may be based on the roles people play, such as mechanics, doctors, and teachers. Early schemata often reflect sex roles and classify behavior by its appropriateness for boys or girls. Categories of behavior may also be differentiated according to behavior settings, such as church, playground, and restaurant.

As time passes, these early schemata are constantly modified. The church schema may be enlarged to include club meetings; the restaurant schema may be enlarged to include behavior appropriate for a dinner guest at a friend's house; the sex-role schema may be split into several subcategories to cover behavior appropriate for different types of girls, different types of boys. Keeping in mind the problem of the match, it is important to broaden children's social experience, but not too suddenly. After the child learns to read and listen and watch television, this enlargement of schemata can proceed symbolically as well as through actual experience.

The possibilities for organizing information about one's world and the people in it become more numerous as growth continues. One often possesses several schemata that might be used in dealing with a new situation. When Billy first goes to summer camp, for example, it is not at all clear whether the camp is a kind of school, a kind of playground, or a kind of party. Different children meet the challenge of a new situation in different ways, some accommodating an existing schema to include new aspects or components, others developing an altogether new schema with its own characteristic shape. The construction and utilization of schemata involve choices, often choices of which neither child nor parents are aware.

Many sorts of choices confront the growing child. Which skills should be practiced? Which social group should be cultivated? Which books should be read? Some of these choices are especially important because they start the child out on one path of life rather than another. Mental health specialists have had much to say about the need for clear life goals. Perhaps a better metaphor would be *direction* rather than goal. It is easier to judge whether one is moving in the direction in which one wishes to go than to formulate just what the goal of the journey is. In our kind of society it is generally agreed that it is better to have individuals making the direction-setting choices themselves than to have those choices made for them. What parents, teachers, and friends of the child can do is to make sure the child experiences a rich variety of alternative situations, so that choices can be informed, not accidental. Daycare centers, nursery schools and kindergartens, summer camps, music lessons, trips abroad, and volunteer work are some ways of providing such experience. There are many others. Adults can also help by showing respect for a child's informed choices, not overriding them unless there is some cogent reason for doing so. A little boy who saves up his allowance money and occasional earnings to buy a camera of his own should be allowed to do so, even if it seems like a waste of money to his mother, who argues that there are several old cameras around the house that he could just as well use. If parents can make sure that only acceptable alternatives appear in the child's world, they can avoid having to veto decisions they believe to be harmful. This, of course, becomes increasingly difficult as the child grows older and as information channels in society become more numerous and complex. As Bandura (1982b) has pointed out, chance encounters may open up possibilities for activities and associations that parents abhor. Should one allow an adolescent girl, for example, to hitchhike through Europe with some of her friends? Sensitivity and responsiveness are needed in dealing with such questions, as is the realization that a child is a separate individual, not *owned* by the parents. Parents are only partly responsible for what their children become and should attempt as much as possible to free themselves from anxiety and guilt about outcomes for which they are not to blame.

Choice making, like other cognitive activities, involves mental structures, or schemata. If in a new situation one had to analyze all the possibilities for action it presents, it would be impossibly difficult to make choices. Indeed, some persons who seek therapy because of chronic indecisiveness seem to have that trouble. What most people do is to apply a kind of schema that I have called a *possibility-processing structure* (Tyler, 1978a). Many kinds of psychological characteristics are included under this label, things such as interest patterns, moral principles, values, ideologies, and self-concepts. Different persons use different combinations of them in making similar choices. Louise, for example, signs up for the high school orchestra because violin playing is the dominant interest of her life. Celia signs up for the orchestra because she values being a well-rounded person and thinks this association with other students in a worthwhile activity is what she needs to become such a person. During the course of development, the individual acquires a repertoire of possibility-processing structures. They are not rigid or immutable. Occasionally one is discarded altogether, as when religious conversion wipes out a pleasure-seeking structure, replacing it with one based on service to God and humanity. More often such structures are transformed gradually through the assimilation and accommodation processes. I have discussed the procedures for teaching children to behave well and the procedures for developing cognitive schemata for storing information as though they were two separate undertakings. It is true that they are based on different research findings obtained by behaviorists and cognitive scientists with quite different assumptions and approaches to their work. However, these two aspects of childrearing are not so clearly separate, and in recent years researchers and theorists representing the two orientations have been moving closer and closer together. Fischer (1980), for example, as mentioned in a previous chapter, is remodeling Piaget's stage theory into a skill theory, in which successive levels are attained through the mastery of successive cognitive skills, acquired in the same way that observable skills like walking or throwing a ball are, through practice and reinforcement.

One research program moving in this direction promises to be of special interest to parents and other custodians of child development. Cognitive psychologists have been interested in problem solving. Shure and Spivack (1978) have been trying to teach what they call "interpersonal cognitive problem-solving skills" (ICPSs) and to show parents and teachers how to do this. There are two essential components of such skills: (1) generating a variety of possible solutions and (2) foreseeing what is likely to happen if each solution is chosen. Explicit instructions for conducting a dialogue with a child in order to set this process in motion are provided. The ICPS procedure is appropriate for a particular kind of cognitive schema, one that controls thinking and actions in relation to other people. The problem of two sisters who are constantly fighting could be approached in this way, or the attempt to modify a "self versus others" schema of a shy and friendless little boy. The concept of multiple possi-

bilities is essential to this procedure. Its success depends strongly on the sheer number of alternative solutions the child is able
to generate.

Special Difficulties with Schools

The principles and procedures I have been discussing so
far apply to all child caretakers, whatever their setting. But
those who work in schools face some special difficulties, many
of them inherent in the very structure of the educational system
we have built. Parents have the advantage of working with one
child at a time, and because every child is different, this is an
important advantage. A teacher who applies the same principle
or uses the same procedure with all twenty-five of the children
of the same age who are in his charge may well be disappointed
in the way it works. These twenty-five children differ far more
from one another in intelligence, previous knowledge, and motivation than our age-grade organization assumes they do. To col-
lect all the six-year-olds in one room, all the ten-year-olds in
another, presenting all members of the age cohort with the same
material to learn, giving them all the same tests, rewarding them
with report-card marks that show how they compared with others on these tests makes no sense at all developmentally. Decades ago, with the advent of standardized achievement tests, it
became apparent that the reading level of individual children in
any one grade varied as much as the *averages* for several grades.
We continue to be shocked by findings that half the students in
a school system score below the average for their age and grade,
even though it is obvious that the way we build our tests pre-
cludes any other result. We are shocked also by reports of illiter-
ate high school graduates, although it should not appear strange
that sitting year after year in classrooms where one's individual
lack of skill is never noticed can hardly be expected to improve
one's reading ability.

Changes once looked on as "progress" in education inten-
sified the problem of individualizing instruction. During earlier
periods, for example, it was customary to narrow the range of
ability in any one grade by speeding up the progress of the faster

learners from grade to grade and slowing down the progress of those who needed more time to master the assigned work. As time passed, educators became reluctant to do this for "social" reasons, although there is no evidence that children of one age differ any less socially than they do intellectually. There is, in fact, a considerable amount of research evidence that brighter children actually develop better socially if they are allowed to accelerate their progress (see Pressey, 1949, for example). Attempts have recently been made to adapt teaching to individual differences within each classroom, using the new computer technology, but they cannot really solve the problem as long as all the children are expected to master the same curriculum and stay in school the same length of time.

The other major shortcoming of our educational system is that it hampers the development of choice making in individuals. Schools, by and large, do not recognize multiple possibilities and encourage students to select those they wish to incorporate in their lives. It is true that secondary schools offer elective courses, but none of them may be devoted to what individuals really want to learn, and the bulk of school time is still spent in activities and assignments required of everybody. Here too "progress" in education has exacerbated the problem. Few citizens or social critics seem to realize that it is less than a century since school attendance was made compulsory in most places. Before that a boy or girl had an option no longer available, simply to drop out of school and find something else to do. Even after elementary education was made compulsory (and a good case can be made that in modern civilized society it is essential), secondary education was optional in most places, and a large proportion of teenagers opted out of it and went to work. We have recently attached such a stigma to the term *dropout* that many persons remain in educational situations that do not contribute in any way to their development. Any program, any curriculum, becomes qualitatively different under different motivation. To make a good program compulsory is often to ruin it.

It seems likely that a thorough reorganization of our whole school system will be needed if schools are to contribute as they should to human development. J. McV. Hunt (1975) points out one place where the system is susceptible to change— namely, the tests we use to evaluate children and programs. He recommends a shift to *criterion-referenced* tests, put together in such a way that each subsection is more advanced than the previous one and presupposes the mastery of the material in the previous one. A criterion-referenced arithmetic test, for example, might begin with the following sequence: (1) one-column addition, (2) one-column subtraction, (3) multicolumn addition, (4) multicolumn subtraction, (5) multiplication tables, and so on. In such a test a child's score would show the teacher what that child already knows and what he or she has yet to learn, making individualized assignments feasible, and children would not be subjected to the stress of being compared with their age mates over and over again. A second recommendation Hunt makes is that classrooms be organized so that a variety of tasks are always available and each child is allowed some choice about what to work on next. In such a situation the teacher "becomes a consultant in learning who counsels her individual students in choice of tasks, helps set the goals of learning in these tasks, and watches for frustrative hangups" (p. 347). Hunt has had less to say about schools at the secondary level, but he thinks that the time allotted to academic subjects should be reduced and boys and girls encouraged to choose and undertake tasks needed for the good of the community.

After examining in detail quantitative and qualitative evidence from an important follow-up in 1975 of youth who had been intensively studied in 1960, I made some specific suggestions for the reorganization of secondary education along these lines (Tyler, 1978b). The objective would be to reduce the amount of compulsion and give individuals more choice about the knowledge and skills they wished to acquire, once they had mastered the basic skills of the elementary school curriculum. This plan calls for the mobilization of all the educational resources of the community, such as the YMCA and YWCA, Boy and Girl Scouts and Four-H Clubs, summer camps and day camps, park programs, teachers of music, art, and dance, businesspersons and skilled technicians willing to instruct apprentices. Only boys and girls who planned to go to college or who had a compelling interest in books and ideas would take a full academic program. For the others the school would serve as a coordinating institution providing skilled counseling, monitoring of progress, and social situations and opportunities. At the end of the secondary period, an individual's diploma would stipulate the skills the person had acquired, so that it would be useful to employers and job applicants.

Other and probably better plans for changes in our school system will undoubtedly be proposed once people realize what the real difficulty is. An awareness of multiple developmental possibilities goes with a recognition that a complex society *needs* people with a variety of skills rather than successive age cohorts that have all been put through the same mill. It is only our familiarity with the present "lockstep" educational system that blinds us to alternative patterns.

Social and Governmental Policies

The full responsibility for bringing up children cannot be carried by individual families and schools. If a new generation is to attain adulthood prepared to meet the challenges our society faces, we must somehow guarantee that *all* children, not just those from fortunate homes and communities, have their basic needs met. To do this requires firm social policies and probably some public funding. Three specific examples come to mind. One is the problem of hunger. Most Americans agree that no child should go hungry, whatever his or her parentage, and social programs like food stamps and school lunches are attempts to meet this need, although they are not altogether adequate. Another problem is illegitimacy and the increasing incidence of teenage pregnancy. Too large a proportion of the coming generation is being reared by very young people with no background or training for parenting—indeed, with no wish to be parents. We have not yet achieved consensus on what should be done about this, but there are social programs to provide contraceptive information, promote celibacy in teenagers, make abortions easily available, or encourage unmarried mothers to release children for adoption. The problem, however, has not been solved. A third serious problem is unemployment among young people, which has reached shocking proportions in the early 1980s. Thousands of boys and girls are in situations in which they are learning to be unproductive citizens for the rest of their lives. The solution is obvious: Put them to work; there is plenty of work to be done. But how to organize this and pay for it is at present not obvious.

I have highlighted only three of the areas in which public policy must supplement private action by families, neighbor-hoods, and schools. There are many others, such as divorce, child abuse, drugs, deaths from automobile accidents. What I would like to emphasize is that there are multiple possibilities for dealing with such social issues. Instead of arguing endlessly over the merits of a plan someone is proposing, we would do well to seek other solutions and try several alternatives. There are many paths to productive maturity, but they all have cer-tain features in common. In a democracy we must make sure that these features appear in the habitats of all children.

CHAPTER 9

Helping Troubled People

❖ ❖ ❖ ❖ ❖ ❖ ❖ ❖ ❖ ❖ ❖ ❖

Of all the ways in which psychology has been brought to bear on human affairs, the largest professional specialty is clinical psychology, the treatment of psychological problems and malfunctions. In each generation, there are always some persons who are unable to cope with life's complexities. In every culture and in every historical epoch, there have been special people whose business it was to help them—witch doctors, priests, physicians, and in our society psychiatrists and psychologists.

Some of the more serious difficulties are so conspicuous that they cannot be ignored. We call them *psychoses* and classify many kinds of bizarre behavior under this label. One psychotic patient sits immobile in a corner, moving her lips in what appears to be a conversation with a nonexistent companion. Such a patient may even commit murder in obedience to the voice she alone hears. Another psychotic patient may storm around the room, breaking up furniture, throwing papers out the window, shouting obscenities at anyone who tries to stop him. Another may suffer from profound depression that completely eliminates interest in anything or anybody and slows all vital functions and thinking processes until they almost cease altogether. A catalogue of psychotic manifestations could be continued indefinitely.

The malfunctions we label *neuroses* do not produce complete breakdown but are characterized by extreme suffering and impairment of the person's productivity and adaptability. There are, for example, depressions not so severe as the one described above but in which the patient is profoundly unhappy and hopeless, unable to see any good in self or circumstances, yet still going through the motions of doing his job from day to day, limping along the dark path of life. Another person may be crippled by an extreme fear of high places or crowds or open spaces, so that she never leaves her house. Worse still are the anxiety states, in which there may be no particular thing or situation that the person fears but in which the threat is everywhere, inescapable, intolerable. Some people are plagued by physical symptoms for which no physical cause can be discovered, such as ulcers, heart irregularities, or headaches. A complete list of the neurotic manifestations for which troubled people have sought treatment would be very long.

In addition to the psychoses and neuroses, there are all sorts of other psychological malfunctions and problems. Some show themselves in relationships with other people, as when a husband and wife who have always been considered to be completely normal find themselves at each other's throats, figuratively speaking. Some difficulties show up during the adolescent period, when boys and girls are unable to negotiate the identity crisis Erikson has written about and find themselves rootless and lost, unable to steer their own lives down paths of their own choosing. Some people realize that they are drinking too much, eating too much, or smoking too much but are unable to stop. Still others develop more serious addictions to expensive legal or illegal drugs and commit crimes in order to obtain them. There are children who get completely out of control of families, schools, or even courts. The sad inventory of things for which people seek psychological help is a long one.

Multiplicity characterizes not only the conditions for which people seek help but also the methods used in helping them. A book by Kanfer and Goldstein (1975) entitled *Helping People Change* discusses twelve major therapeutic approaches, but each of these has many subdivisions, and new ones are being proposed every year. It seems especially important that help seekers and help providers realize that there are multiple possibilities. The same techniques do not work for everybody.

Sundberg, Taplin, and Tyler (1983) suggest that all these diverse helping activities can be classified under four major orientations. Each of the four approaches has its own history, its own theories, its own body of research evidence to draw on. The four orientations are (1) curative, (2) learning, (3) growth, and (4) ecological.

Curative Orientation

The curative orientation is the oldest, the most prestigious, and probably the most frequent approach to therapy. Psychologists often refer to it as the *medical model,* because it is patterned after medical practice. Its leading practitioners and spokespersons are, in fact, physicians who have specialized in psychiatry, but many other kinds of helpers, such as psychologists, social workers, nurses, and paraprofessionals of various sorts, also accept it without question.

According to this way of thinking, it makes sense to start with a thorough diagnosis, consisting of a detailed description of the patient's complaints, and an analysis, at least tentative, of the causes of the condition. Treatment should, if possible, be directed at these causes, although alleviation of symptoms, attempts to make the patient more comfortable, may be undertaken while deeper sources are being probed. During the early years of this century, psychologists were brought into treatment teams mainly for their diagnostic skills, because they had tools available for assessing an individual's intelligence and personality characteristics and even for making shrewd guesses about whether brain damage was present and, if so, where the lesion would probably be found. During those years, psychiatrists handled the therapy. But as time passed, psychologists became less and less content to play an ancillary role and contended that they had useful knowledge about how *change* takes place, knowledge that qualified them to be therapists as well as diagnosticians. Bitter struggles took place over this issue, struggles that still continue in some quarters, but in general the right of psychologists to practice psychotherapy has been recognized. Other workers in mental health professions, such as social workers, nurses, clergymen, and trained volunteers, are also involved to some extent in therapy.

The goal of many medically trained psychiatrists, to identify a definite physical cause for every psychological malfunction, has not been realized. It was tremendously encouraging, a century or so ago, when general paresis, a degenerative psychosis, was shown to result from syphilitic infection. But although a great deal of research has been done since then, physical causes for most other kinds of psychosis have not shown up. Take, for example, that most puzzling of all mental diseases, schizophrenia, characterized by a shattering of the whole personality, so that emotions do not match situations, thinking is disorganized and bizarre, and motivation to carry on life's normal activities is lacking. Physiological concomitants have been found, but some of these abnormalities may be the result, rather than the cause, of the breakdown. The condition tends to run in families, but not all children of schizophrenic parents are afflicted, and we do not know why. Nevertheless, drug treatment seems to work in many cases, thus strengthening the case for a medical approach. Another widely used medical treatment is shock therapy, against which there has been a considerable public outcry in recent years.

The curative approach characterizes much psychological as well as physical and pharmaceutical treatment. It was Freud who brought to the world's attention the fact that it is possible for people to be mentally ill without any flaws in physical mechanisms, because of the directions in which experience has channeled their development. As discussed earlier, he considered the child's relationship to the parents during the earliest years crucially important for its channeling effect. Because so much

of experience is unconscious, diagnosis of deep-lying psychological causes is extremely difficult. The kind of therapy Freud
pioneered, psychoanalysis, was aimed at the root causes of malfunctioning, but they could be diagnosed only gradually, in the
course of treatment. Through free association, dream analysis,
and skillful interpretations by the analyst, the patient learned to
make sense of apparently irrational feelings and actions, and in
the relationship with the therapist he or she relived the earlier
situations and broke out of the channel in which he or she had
been immobilized. Needless to say, psychoanalysis is a long and
expensive process, and it does not always work, but many suf-
ferers are still willing to undergo it for the relief of intolerable
states of mind and the self-understanding it brings. It has always
been used more with neurotics than with psychotics, although
some therapists have reported good results with schizophrenics
and severely depressed patients as well.

Obviously a complete psychoanalysis lasting months or
years and costing several thousand dollars is not for everybody.
Much more frequently found in present practice is *psychody-
namic therapy,* a short treatment based on Freud's ideas. Therapists encourage and deal with transference. They employ various techniques to minimize the inevitable resistance that patients
generate against the recovery of painful unconscious material.
They make use of interpretation—that is, psychological statements that go just a little beyond what patients have actually
expressed—in order to enable patients to achieve insight. At the
end there is a period of *working through,* in which insights are
applied to all the varied circumstances that patients face. Psycho-
dynamic therapy takes several weeks rather than several years to
complete, and many people have used it to help in extricating
themselves from a morass of anxiety and motivational conflicts.

There are dozens of short therapies based to a greater or
lesser extent on psychoanalytic ideas, in that they seek the
causes of psychological difficulties in emotional experiences individuals have undergone and attempt to remove or counteract
these causes. As explained earlier, the notion that it is the very
earliest experience that is all-important has been abandoned or
at least modified as research results have come in. Thus, ther-

apists no longer consider it essential that memories of what happened during the first two or three years be recovered. Traumatic experiences can occur at any age, as attempts to help battle-scarred veterans have demonstrated. During and since Freud's lifetime, different theorists and practitioners have concentrated on particular kinds of experience, kinds of people, or periods of life. Jung, for example, emphasized the later periods and paid more attention than Freud did to the functions of myths and symbols and to the creative aspects of the unconscious. Adler made major contributions to the problems of children and emphasized the social aspects of motivation and the anxiety produced by deep-lying inferiority feelings. Horney analyzed and classified the neurotic needs that produce emotional conflicts and the therapeutic procedures by means of which their urgency could be reduced. Human nature is so complex that every therapist discovers new possible sources of suffering and stagnation. To discover them and then to remove or counteract them—this is the aim of all the therapies I have classified under the curative label. They all have their successes and their failures. None of them works for everybody, and each of them works differently for different therapists and different patients.

Later in the chapter research on the evaluation of therapy will be discussed. At this point it is necessary only to point out that the basic assumption that all psychological difficulties are illnesses and should be treated as such is not grounded in fact. There are other ways of looking at such difficulties. The concept of mental illness has been around for a long time, but only during the last century or so has it been the dominant way of approaching the problems. In some centuries, demon possession was the preferred explanation, and it seemed reasonable to execute witches on the assumption that their peculiarities meant they had sold their souls to Satan.

We would not want to return to such assumptions, but it is important to recognize that there are other alternatives. It is true that confinement in a mental hospital is preferable to being thrown into jail, run out of town on a rail, or burned at the stake. Regarding troubled people as ill makes for kindness, compassion, and efforts to help, but in our time the unfortunate aspects of this assumption are becoming apparent, and more and more voices are being raised against the "myth of mental illness." It can become a way of dealing with unorthodox behavior of all sorts, as the present concern over the hospitalization of dissidents in the Soviet Union illustrates. It can lead to dependence, irresponsibility, and the loss of basic rights and human dignity. It is not only the psychotics in hospital back wards who pay this price. Maladjusted people who spend year after year and thousands on thousands of dollars trying out different brands of therapy, and who come to depend upon it for their only satisfactions, are also casualties. Another inadequacy of the curative orientation is that it focuses on the individual personality and neglects the larger systems that may be more in need of change than individuals are.

Many psychologists would like to focus on the *prevention* of psychopathology rather than its cure. Such an effort calls for major changes in schools, communities, and workplaces and for social supports to enable families to function better. The dominance of the curative orientation has affected the delivery of psychological services in ways that make it difficult to accomplish this. For example, our mental health clinics and our private practitioners are increasingly being reimbursed for their services through payments by insurance companies. These are made only for the treatment of patients with diagnosed illnesses. Consequently, it is difficult to make a living doing community work or lobbying for legislative changes. We know that unemployment is a major source of psychological difficulties at this time, but mental health workers cannot do much to combat it. Thus, finding alternatives to the curative approach is of some practical importance.

Learning Orientation

Ever since psychology got started as an independent discipline, more than a hundred years ago, the problem of how people learn has been intensively studied. Controlled observation in laboratories and observations in schools and industrial training programs have produced a considerable body of knowledge.

Much of this is applicable to the treatment of psychological problems and malfunctions.

Out of Pavlov's finding that a dog that heard a bell ring just as it took a mouthful of food would after a few trials salivate whenever it heard the bell came the concept of the *conditioned response*. Knowing that a response made naturally to one stimulus could be transferred to another, no matter how inappropriate, had exciting implications for psychologists. Take this patient with an irrational fear of animals, for example. Could it have originated in a situation in which someone nearby shot off a gun just as a harmless cat was approaching, so that the natural response to the shot had been transferred to the cat? Watson, often known as the founder of behaviorism, tested this possibility with a baby named Albert, demonstrating that a fear of furry animals could be instilled in a person by making a loud noise coincide with the animal's approach. Could it be that the anxiety Freud and his followers had found to be the soil out of which neurosis grew was created by such incidents? And if so, could not what had been learned be unlearned if suitable situations could be designed?

Other psychologists, most notably Skinner, demonstrated how important *reinforcement* was in learning. Any chance bit of behavior that is rewarded is likely to occur again, and if rewarding consequences continue to follow it, the behavior becomes habitual. How many of the bizarre behaviors we see in psychotics could have been unwittingly brought into existence in this way? Other researchers showed that the perceptual schemata and cognitive structures built into individual personalities can take shapes that produce impasses in attempts to adapt to one's world. Many other kinds of research discussed in earlier chapters were picked up by clinical psychologists and used as the basis for new theories about deviance and therapy. Psychologists found new ways of treating conditions that had been called mental illness. The principal way in which the learning orientation differs from the curative orientation is that instead of regarding the things the troubled person does, says, and feels as *symptoms* of some invisible underlying condition, it considers them to be the problem itself. The behavior therapist reasons, "Somewhere along the line this person has learned some unfortunate or inadequate habits. Let's see what we can do to help him or her learn some new ones." Each major learning theory generates its own system of therapy.

One of the first of these to be worked out in some detail was Wolpe's *systematic desensitization,* based on Pavlovian conditioned response principles. It is widely used in the treatment of neurotic fears and anxieties. The first step is for the patient to produce a list of fear-producing situations and arrange the items in order from the least to the most disturbing. The second step is for the therapist to train the patient in relaxation procedures or some other kind of behavior incompatible with fear. The third step, which takes up the rest of the therapy sessions, is to condition the relaxation response to the stimuli that now initiate the fear response, in vividly imagined situations, beginning with the least disturbing situation in the patient's hierarchy and gradually proceeding to the most disturbing. Many variations of this basic plan have been tried out, all with the purpose of replacing discomfort in the situations the person finds most disabling.

Another main branch of learning therapy is based on Skinner's concepts rather than Pavlov's. It is especially useful in dealing with behavior for which no *one* initiating stimulus can be identified. The bad behavior of children often falls into this category. The first step in this procedure is a careful analysis of what the person is actually *doing* and how these actions are currently being reinforced. Discontinuing such reinforcement altogether causes the behavior to be *extinguished.* But this may be a slow process and may be difficult or impossible. Take, for example, the case of a child throwing temper tantrums that involve banging his head against a hard wall, a behavior reinforced by being picked up and held. What is usually necessary is a second step, in which a more appropriate form of behavior is identified and reinforced. Several techniques are now available for producing a new kind of behavior. The process called *shaping,* widely used in animal training, simply means reinforcing successive approximations to the desired act. With children it is usually more efficient to have a *model* demonstrate the desired behavior or to tell the child what one wants him or her to do.

Reinforcing the child's new behavior builds it into his or her repertoire and makes the undesirable behavior unnecessary.

An outline like the foregoing makes the task look much simpler than it is. To design a plan for inducing the occurrence of actions, providing effective reinforcements, and monitoring the whole undertaking calls for a great deal of ingenuity as well as familiarity with behavioral learning research and theory. With such plans, hyperactive children have been trained to settle down and do their schoolwork; mentally retarded children have been taught to read and write; lonely children have been taught to enter into playground games. Behavior therapy is for adults as well as children. Groups organized according to its principles help participants break the smoking habit, lose weight, and become more assertive. Weekly weigh-ins are powerful reinforcers for people who really want to lose weight, and the satisfaction a timid woman gets from stating an opinion reinforces assertive behavior. Life has been made tolerable for patients in back wards of mental hospitals by a system called a *token economy,* in which a token is given to a patient every time he or she acts in a "normal," socially acceptable way. Tokens are exchangeable within the hospital for treats and privileges, so that they serve as immediate reinforcers. Parents have successfully used the same system with incorrigible children. In general, the practice of behavior modification in homes, schools, and hospitals involves ignoring undesirable behavior and using reinforcement to strengthen the tendency to do the right things.

Behavior therapy, as practiced at the beginning, turned out to have one serious disadvantage. The changed behavior often did not *generalize* to different situations. For example, a child who had learned to pick up toys and put them away in the playroom of a clinic might still be as untidy as ever at home. A former smoker who had learned not to smoke at home might find herself lighting up again when she went to a convention in a distant city. The relapse rate for persons treated in detoxification centers and drug addiction clinics is notoriously high once clients return to their home communities. Such situational specificity is not an insoluble problem, but it does require attention in the designing of therapy programs. The trouble is that when a response is reinforced in a particular context, some of the features of that context function as *discriminative* cues to what the response should be. Discovering this has led to research on *stimulus control,* the results of which can be applied in designing therapy programs. A perceptive therapist identifies some of the discriminative stimuli and arranges for them to be present in the situations to which patients return. For example, dieters may be trained to eat only in a particular place at home and at set times, not to talk or watch television while eating, and to clear excess food from their plates directly into the garbage pail as soon as they have finished eating, thus reducing markedly the number of incidental cues that lead to overeating.

The learning approach to psychotherapy includes *thinking* modification as well as behavior modification. With increasing interest in cognitive psychology has come the development of therapies aiming to help people change the patterns of thinking out of which their psychological difficulties are assumed to grow. Cognitive therapists believe that malfunctioning arises from wrong ideas, wrong attitudes, and wrong expectations and that these can be replaced with sounder ones through a learning process. An active spokesman for this point of view is Ellis (1962), who advocates what he calls *rational-emotive* therapy. It differs not only from the behaviorist variety but from the psychoanalytic variety as well, in that it is based on the assumption that faulty emotions follow thought rather than precede it, so that emotional problems can best be changed by bringing about changes in thinking. Ellis has listed eleven typical irrational beliefs frequently encountered in therapy seekers. Some are about the self, such as the "idea that it is a dire necessity for a human being to be loved or approved by virtually every other person in his community" (p. 61). Others are about other people, such as the "idea that certain people are bad, wicked, or villainous and that they should be severely blamed and punished for their villainy" (p. 65). Still others are about how one ought to act in the world as one believes it is, such as the "idea that one should be dependent on others and needs someone stronger than oneself on whom to rely" (p. 80). During therapy sessions Ellis identifies and points out to clients what their wrong thoughts are and then has them imagine concrete situations and the ways they might deal with them if they thought about them in a different way. Imagining situations is a technique similar to Wolpe's, discussed earlier, but Ellis follows it with training in active coping rather than relaxation. Other cognitive therapists recommend other specific procedures, but active coping through improved thinking is characteristic of them all.

I have discussed behavioral and cognitive therapies as if they were two completely different kinds of effort to help people with psychological difficulties. In practice they are not so clearly separable. In research and in practical application, the two ways of working have been coming closer and closer together. A synthesis called *cognitive behavior therapy* is beginning to emerge. Behaviorists now admit that undesirable actions can result from faulty beliefs and expectations. Cognitivists can regard the thinking strategies they teach as skills to be learned according to the same principles as other skills. In any particular case, whether the aim should be to change the behavior or to change the thinking depends on many factors, including the client's personality and past history, the availability of resources, the attitudes of other persons in the individual's habitat, and the competencies of the therapist. The Shure and Spivack (1978) program to train children in interpersonal cognitive problem-solving skills, discussed in the previous chapter, is a good example of cognitive behavior therapy, combining aspects of behavior modification with training in right thinking. It is worth noting that the most essential part of this training is to generate a number of *possible* solutions to the problem and foresee as many *possible* consequences of each as one can. The concept of multiple possibilities holds a central place in cognitive behavior therapy.

One advantage that all the learning therapies have over the curative therapies is that a larger assortment of therapists can be trained to practice them. One need not be a licensed psychiatrist or psychologist; teachers, social workers, physicians, ministers, school counselors, and volunteer workers can learn to help people function better. Admittedly such breadth of application has its dangers. People may try to bring about changes in other people's lives without having any clear idea of what they are doing, and they may do harm as well as good. But through education, what psychologists have learned about learning can be taught. To spread the knowledge as widely as possible is one of the major responsibilities of scientists and professionals.

Growth Orientation

The growth orientation, which made its appearance somewhat more recently than the two already discussed, has as its purpose the facilitation of natural psychological development. Jung's ideas (Campbell, 1971) have entered into this stream of thinking, especially his assumption that psychological growth does not stop with the attainment of adulthood but continues throughout life. A more influential figure was Rogers, whose books *Counseling and Psychotherapy* (1942) and *Client-Centered Therapy* (1951) became almost the bibles of the new movement. This orientation has been characterized as follows: "Therapy aims to *release the potential for growth.* A basic growth tendency in every person is postulated, a tendency toward maturity and integration. Unfortunate circumstances or adverse influences can block or temporarily reverse this process but cannot destroy it completely. What therapy aims to do is to remove these obstacles, whatever they are, and allow the person to start growing again along the lines of his own unique pattern. The psychotherapist should not be thought of as a mechanic, locating and repairing defects in a piece of equipment, but as more like a gardener, providing light, nutrients, and moisture to stimulate a plant intrinsically disposed to grow" (Sundberg, Tyler, and Taplin, 1973, p. 294).

I noted in an earlier section that psychoanalysis also emphasizes development. But where analysts assume that the early years are all-important and that early periods must be relived through the transference if personality reorganization is to occur, growth therapists assume that personality development continues throughout life and that personality change is not limited by what happened during the first few years. Personality is so complex that some channels of growth are always open to an individual.

The main responsibility of the therapist is to create a climate facilitating growth, a climate encouraging openness, self-exploration, and confrontation of feelings. It is the client who must carry out the exploration, achieve the insights, consider possible changes. A therapist who is too active, offering interpretations and advice, is a handicap, not a help. What matters is what the therapist *is* rather than what he or she says or thinks. In a 1957 paper, Rogers analyzed "the necessary and sufficient conditions for therapeutic change." Truax and Carkhuff (1967) elaborated the three core concepts Rogers had presented and used them as a foundation for an influential system of practice and research. The three necessary and sufficient conditions, with the names Truax and Carkhuff gave them, are (1) accurate empathy, (2) nonpossessive warmth, and (3) genuineness. Accurate empathy means being sensitive to feelings and meanings expressed by a client, being able to see things from the client's point of view, and communicating one's understanding to the client. Rogers called this quality "empathic understanding." Nonpossessive warmth means being able to accept clients without evaluating or criticizing anything they say about themselves or their past actions. Rogers' name for this quality was "unconditional positive regard." Genuineness means that whatever the therapist says or does must be sincere, not simulated. Rogers called this quality "self-congruence" to bring out the fact that a genuine person must be in touch with all aspects of his or her own organism. These essential qualities can be developed through training, and one need not be a psychologist or psychiatrist to learn them.

A salient characteristic of the growth approach is emphasis on the *relationship* of client and therapist. Many things have been shown to influence this. Goldstein (1975) has given us a detailed discussion of relationship-enhancing factors. The initial attraction of client toward therapist depends to some extent on how the process of therapy is structured for the client in the first interview. Client respect for the therapist rests on evidence that the helper is an expert; diplomas, degrees, and so on, inconspicuously displayed, have some effect, as do greetings, seating positions, and other minor things. Empathy has been studied by analyzing therapists' responses to what clients say. Some express empathy clearly; others do not.

As the years passed, growth therapy was increasingly practiced in group situations, leading in the 1960s and 1970s to the human potential movement. Rogers became highly involved in *encounter groups,* viewed as the major vehicle for the release of human potential. Such groups are less popular now than in 1970, but they are still helping many people to develop richer, more adequate personalities. There has been a considerable amount of gimmickry and bizarre behavior in the encounter movement during its heyday, but its basis was essentially the same as that of all growth therapy. Rogers (1980) describes the process. The leader first of all creates a climate of safety, in which participants find it possible to reveal their feelings. Expressing feelings and having them accepted by other group members enables them to drop some of their defenses and accept their total selves, including the potential for change. New possibilities for specific changes emerge, and feedback from fellow members of the group, whom one has come to trust completely, helps with the evaluation of such possibilities. Finally what one learns about self and others carries over into all one's relationships with family, friends, and associates. Obviously this is the ideal, and groups do not always attain it. Opportunities for things to go wrong are multiplied when several persons are interacting. But Rogers (1980) still believes that the prospects for constructive change through groups are very bright. Recently his own efforts have been directed to large groups, consisting of strangers brought together for workshops only a few days long. He reports that even within these limits the same process occurs as in smaller, more intimate groups.

Ecological Approach

The ecological approach is the newest of the four orientations and does not yet have as many specific concepts and techniques as the others. It is grounded in general systems theory and holds promise for the prevention as well as the relief of psychological difficulties. Fundamental to this approach is the realization that an individual is part of larger systems and that what looks like malfunctioning in the individual may be malfunction in the way one of these larger systems is working. The professional person who wishes to help must first decide what the relevant system is. Is it the family, the school class, the work group? The intervener then analyzes this system, seeking to discover how the physical and psychological environment affects the participants, how they interact with one another, and what resources and interpersonal supports the system provides. Possibilities for reorganization and change are then considered, places where small and feasible changes in one component might lead to large changes in the whole.

The one kind of system to which this approach has most often been taken is the family, and in this one area there is a sizable body of knowledge to draw on. For a childless couple, therapy takes the form of what is generally called marriage counseling, but this is being practiced in the case of unmarried couples and even homosexual couples as well. Whichever partner makes the initial contact, the therapist makes an effort to involve both of them so that the focus of attention can be on their interaction rather than on the inadequacies of either of them. Sometimes other, more peripheral participants are brought in, such as in-laws, neighbors, and friends (always with the permission of the couple who are the clients, of course). Counseling of this sort is often done in groups so that new opportunities for observation of interactions and new sources of support are made available.

When a family includes children, the process of analyzing and intervening is more complex—and also perhaps more urgent, since the same kinds of psychological difficulties, untreated, are likely to appear generation after generation in families. It has been shown that this occurs, for example, in cases of child abuse. There is no standard catalogue of techniques for a therapist to turn to in trying to reorganize a family system, but it is essential that one create a situation in which interactions can be observed. This may mean interviews in which the whole family participates, or perhaps visits to the home at a time when all members of the family are there. As therapy proceeds, the parents may be taught principles of behavior modification, parents and children may be given roles to play, or different family members may be assigned tasks to carry out at home. The sensitivity and creativity of the therapist are all-important.

There is even less accumulated knowledge about applying the ecological approach to school or work situations. Perhaps improvisation rather than trained skills will always characterize these efforts. The most significant benefit coming from the focus on ecology may be the changes that are taking place in our thinking, the realizations that the roots of individual and social problems are often to be found in the way larger systems function and that such systems can be changed.

Multiple Possibilities in Psychotherapy

We are all potential consumers of psychotherapy, and it is important for us to know that there are many ways in which it can be provided. To some extent, the selection of a promising approach depends on the nature of the difficulty for which help is sought. For example, patients suffering from serious psychosis, such as schizophrenia, are usually candidates for the curative approach. But even in such cases other approaches have been tried. Learning situations can be set up to change the patients' habit patterns enough to enable them to cope with life's demands. The growth approach was applied with some success by Rogers and his associates (1967) in the treatment of schizophrenics. Others, following the ecological approach, have organized groups of patients to live together, working with and supporting one another, outside the institution in which they had been hospitalized. Patients, or their families if the patients are completely disabled, have some latitude in deciding what kind of treatment they want.

People with less serious difficulties, from neuroses on down to examination anxiety, have more choices. They may be helped by medication or undertake psychoanalysis, both curative treatments, arrange for individual learning therapy aimed at eliminating troublesome symptoms, sign up for groups designed to facilitate growth, or participate with other members of their families in ecological therapy.

Evaluation research has consistently failed to demonstrate the *general* superiority of any one brand. In fact, the question "Does *any* kind of psychotherapy do any good?" was not answered positively until recently. As early as 1952 Eysenck compared groups of neurotics who had received treatment with those who had not and found that in both cases about two thirds of the subjects were rated a year or two later "Recovered" or "Much improved" and that the other third were rated "Not improved" or "Left treatment." (The kinds of therapy available then were, of course, much more limited than they are now.) Almost thirty years later Smith, Glass, and Miller (1980) were able to put together the results of more than 400 outcome studies and to demonstrate a clear difference between treated and untreated groups. But they could find no evidence that different types of therapy produced different amounts of benefit, whether administered to individuals or groups, by therapists with much or with little experience, or for short or long periods. Such results should not be interpreted to mean that those rated "Not improved" are hopeless cases who must resign themselves to suffering all their lives. The results of outcome studies are equally compatible with the conclusion that some people do not benefit because they received a kind of treatment that was not right for them.

A salient phenomenon of our time is the proliferation of groups composed simply of persons with similar problems, groups designed to enable troubled individuals to help one another cope with their circumstances without seeking trained professional assistance. Alcoholics Anonymous was the earliest of these and is still the best known, but there are dozens of others made up of fat people, over- and undersized people, smokers trying to shake the habit, divorced mothers, parents of retarded children—the list could be continued on and on. Especially for people whose disabilities are limited to one or a few problems and who know what it is that troubles them, these groups open up new possibilities for improving human lives. Such groups can be seen as an outgrowth of the learning and developmental thinking about therapy. Participants learn from one another, and together they create a climate of understanding and support that facilitates growth.

Because there are so many possibilities for assistance with psychological problems, a person seeking help should first of all try to find one that feels right for himself or herself. This may not be easy. There are as yet no dependable techniques for matching individuals with therapies, and most professional therapists are trained and experienced in only one approach. But in spite of these limitations, for therapists and clients to realize the multiplicity of the therapy possibilities can be an advantage. One need not give up hope of improvement.

CHAPTER 10

Directing and Controlling
One's Own Life

❖ ❖ ❖ ❖ ❖ ❖ ❖ ❖ ❖ ❖ ❖ ❖

The most valuable contribution the concept of multiple possibilities can make is to help people manage their own lives more successfully. Why should not psychological knowledge and skills be acquired and used by everybody rather than only by specialized therapists and consultants? In his presidental address to the American Psychological Association, George Miller (1969) made a suggestion that has been quoted again and again —namely, that it is our responsibility to find ways to "give psychology away." A serious effort to do this is now being made.

Psychotherapy Moves Toward Self-Management

Therapists, particularly behavior therapists, have been incorporating self-management concepts and procedures into their thinking and practice. Although people experiencing the more serious psychological disabilities will probably always require professional treatment, a considerable fraction of the people consulting psychotherapists are not really "ill" in this sense. They complain of such things as persistent anxiety, uncontrollable fears, marital and family difficulties, lack of self-confidence, depression, boredom, and a general feeling of meaninglessness. Many therapists who have helped people plan programs to deal with such conditions have come to realize that the responsibility for carrying out these programs is in the hands of the clients themselves, and often they themselves can formulate the treatment plans if they understand the fundamental principles of learning and personality change.

In the case of behavior therapy, these fundamentals are straightforward and fairly simple. First of all, there must be a careful analysis, quantitative if possible, of what it is in the person's life that needs changing. If, for example, the problem is a vague but persistent feeling of depression, the initial assessment may call for an hour-by-hour checking of one's moods carried on for several days and a description of the situations preceding or accompanying the changes. Having identified certain kinds of situations that seem to be related to the feeling, one proceeds to the second step, selecting features of these situations that are susceptible to change. There are always multiple possibilities at this stage for changes ranging from a move to a completely different milieu or habitat to a simple strategy for avoiding a particular companion. For some kinds of problems a milieu change is all that is needed for a solution, but more frequently a change in the person's behavior is called for as well. The depressed person in our example may need to seek out and participate in activities that give pleasure and to reschedule his or her life to include them. To do this may require some reduction in a crippling shyness. The third step a person must take is to set in motion a process of self-reinforcement that will produce and strengthen the new habits. In accordance with Skinner's concept of shaping, small steps toward the desired goal may be reinforced at the beginning. A shy young man, for example, may decide to reward himself with a candy bar each time he telephones a girl for a date, whether her reply is positive or negative. A record of an increasing number of calls made from week to week indicates progress, and eventually someone is almost certain to accept his invitation. Once this happens, the arbitrary candy-bar reinforcement can be replaced by the pleasure the association provides. Ideally, this is the way the process of behavior change works. If the first plan does not, there are, fortunately, multiple possibilities for reinforcement and shaping, so that a different plan can be put into operation. Many behavior therapists now see their task as that of helping people develop their own plans and monitor their own progress in carrying them out. Parents are learning how to control unruly children; fat people are changing their dietary habits; smokers are giving up cigarettes; timid people are becoming more assertive, mostly or entirely through their own efforts.

It is not only behavior therapy that is being adapted for self-management. Procedures that are used in some of the affective and motivational therapies are also available for use by people with problems even without the assistance of professional therapists. The most pre-eminent among these, psychoanalysis, is not a *self*-change process, although Freud, its originator, did carry out a self-analysis. However, many of the separate kinds of clues to understanding that psychoanalysts use can be utilized by anyone who chooses to observe them systematically. We all dream and can try to interpret our own dreams. Similarly, our own interpretations of daydreams, fantasies, and slips of the tongue can help make us aware of how we really feel and what we really want. People can reduce troublesome tension by learning techniques of progressive relaxation from good books on the subject now available. More esoteric techniques like meditation can also be learned from books.

The cognitive therapies, which focus attention at the outset on the ways people think rather than how they feel, are also being adapted for use by troubled persons themselves. Problem-solving techniques that have proved their worth in experiments as well as therapy are available to anyone who wishes to try them. There are multiple possibilities in the realm of assumptions and beliefs as well as actions. These are fitted together into a coherent *script*, and it is possible for a person to change his or her life by replacing one script with another. What stands in our way is the failure to recognize that there are other scripts that combine the same facts. A depressed college student, for example, may be living by a script like the following:

> I was an illegitimate, rejected child. Mother didn't love me. I never knew my father. People have always avoided me; they never ask me to join them in anything they are doing. I have been a failure at everything I have tried to do. It would have been better if I had never been born. I think constantly about killing myself; there is no reason for me to go on living.

Everything the person knows about his past, present, and future could be organized in a different script if he could only see the possibility. Such an alternative might look like the following:

> I was a "love child." My father was a very intelligent, handsome young man, but his family kept him from marrying my mother because he was only nineteen and she was from a poor family. She was very courageous, however, and decided to have the baby and to keep me. It meant a lot of hard work for her, and of course she didn't have much time to devote to me. But she did the best she could, and I knew she loved me. In some ways it was an advantage for me that I had to be "on my own" at an early age, although it stood in the way of my friendships with other children. We lived in such a poor neighborhood that I didn't want to associate with the other children who lived near me. I always did fairly well with my schoolwork, and I finished high school with a B average. Right now I'm out of a job, but if times pick up, I know I can get my old job back or one just as good, and if I can get some new clothes and move to a better apartment, I think I can make some new friends and put the unhappiness of the past behind me.

I'm going to take some college courses and study
to be an accountant.

Once one has generated a new script for one's life, the
construction of a program for self-change out of components
from many systems of therapy is a feasible task. Books are now
appearing designed to teach people how to do this. One by
Rudestan (1980), for example, presents what he calls the ABC
model (affective, behavioral, cognitive) and explains in considerable detail how to apply twenty procedures drawn from these
three main varieties of therapy.

Intentional Change

Another recent book (Tough, 1982) carries the idea
somewhat further. The author is interested in the process of intentional change for people in general, not just for those need-
ing therapy. He presents evidence that this is far more prevalent
than psychologists have been assuming. He reports the results
of a survey of 150 American, British, and Canadian men and
women. The interviewers asked them to recall the most important intentional change they had made in their lives during the
previous two years. Four areas accounted for 75 percent of the
changes: (1) jobs, career, and training, (2) human relationships,
emotions, and self-perceptions, (3) enjoyable activities, and (4)
residence location. Job changes were most frequently mentioned. The proportions of changes classified in the different
categories did not differ from country to country. Most subjects
reported that the changes had improved their lives to a considerable extent.

The researchers were most interested in how these people
had gone about making the changes. They found that the great
majority had planned them and carried them out on their own
without help from anyone. Very few had consulted professionals or read self-help books. Tough writes, "I am struck by the
wide variety of techniques, approaches, psychologies, learning
principles, and learning styles that the same person will use
from one change to another. One key to successful changes may

be the person's wide repertoire of strategies from which to choose in particular situations" (p. 63). When they needed advice or support, these people most frequently turned to nonprofessionals rather than to psychologists or counselors. The self-help groups mentioned in the previous chapter were sometimes used, but more frequently the helper was a family member or a friend. "Some are coworkers, acquaintances, bartenders, hairdressers, or even strangers" (p. 66). How many of us on long train or plane rides have listened, often unwillingly, to the stories of people in trouble who are trying to make decisions!

Tough points out implications of these findings for professional practice. If psychologists followed his suggestions, they would spend less time "treating" individual patients and clients and more time making resources for change readily available for everybody. One useful service would be to provide sound information in accessible places, such as racks in public libraries and offices of social agencies and public officials. Assessment centers might be set up to "help people get in touch with themselves and assist them with life changes, lifelong learning, and general enhancement of coping skills and quality of life" (Sundberg, Snowden, and Reynolds, 1978, p. 208). For providing information about opportunities and resources, learning networks are proving their worth in many communities (Calvert and Draves, 1978). People seeking to bring about changes in their lives need information about which persons in the community are experts in particular areas, about self-help groups, about occupations and jobs that are available, about leisure activities, and about many other things. As Tough explains, a society that disseminates consumer information about automobiles, stereos, insurance, cosmetics, and many other products ought to be able to give sound information about the resources that consumers could draw on in managing their lives. The most important recommendations he makes, and those most likely to be resisted by professional psychologists, have to do with widening the range of human resources from which helpers can be chosen, by relaxing licensing laws and other professional controls. "Ideally people should be able to choose their changes from an excellent variety of possibilities and then should be free to choose from several effective methods or resources. A pluralistic society is tolerant of a wide diversity of changes and paths as long as they do not unduly interfere with anyone else" (p. 97).

The research on which Tough's book is based can be criticized on some counts, most importantly because the samples in the countries were selected on the basis of availability of interviewers in those locations rather than because they were representative of any particular population. At each location the interviewers did attempt to sample the adult population from age twenty-five on up in an unbiased way, drawing names from voter lists and telephone books or knocking on doors at random. The final sample did cover a wide range of ages and social levels, and the fact that the three national samples differed in structure as little as they did suggests that obvious biases had been eliminated. However the research is evaluated, it is the ideas stimulated by the survey that constitute the major contribution Tough's book makes, and it is the ideas that should be considered more than the quantitative results. And they are very challenging.

Role of Choice in Self-Management

What might be questioned with regard to the ideas I have been discussing is their emphasis on *change*. It is too closely tied to our "culture of psychotherapy." Among psychologists there seems to be an implicit assumption that individuals make important choices, decisions, or plans only when they face some psychological problem or difficulty. *Change,* of course, is an ambiguous word. In its broad sense it pervades all of life and is synonymous with what I have called *development.* But as clinicians typically use it, it means the overcoming of some unhappy state of affairs, such as a crippling phobia or overwhelming shyness, or the modification of some unfortunate personality trait like overdependence or general hostility. It is the broader sense of development over time that concerns us here. How can individuals manage their own lives better from year to year, whether they encounter psychological problems or not?

The most fundamental factor is not change but *choice.*

The reason is that possibilities are many, many times as numerous as actualities. Examples are everywhere. A couple conceives
two children, but there are billions of egg/sperm combinations
that could have occurred but did not. (Chance rather than
choice, of course, operates here.) A child learns one language
and sometimes eventually an additional one or even several, but
there are thousands of other languages that might have been
learned instead. (This is partly a matter of the culture into
which the person is born, but choice does play some part.) Out
of the upwards of four billion persons in the world, one individual becomes acquainted with not more than a few hundred and
comes to know only a few dozen even moderately well. Out of
the thousands of places in the world, one person seldom travels
to more than a hundred or so and seldom lives even briefly in
more than a dozen. The earliest selections from the plethora of
possibilities are made for the individual by chance or by other
people, but from childhood on, most of the rest depend to a
greater or lesser extent on the person's own choices. William
James described the transformation of multiple possibilities into
single actualities with exceptional clarity, in the passage cited in
Chapter One about the sculptor extricating one particular statue
from the many possible ones existing in a block of stone.

In another famous passage, James (1890) applies the
same idea to the development of personality:

> I am often confronted by the necessity of
> standing by one of my empirical selves and relin-
> quishing the rest. Not that I would not, if I could,
> be both handsome and fat and well dressed, and a
> great athlete, and make a million a year, be a wit, a
> bon vivant, and a lady-killer, as well as a philos-
> opher; a philanthropist, statesman, warrior, and
> African explorer, as well as a "tone poet" and
> saint. But the thing is simply impossible. The mil-
> lionaire's work would run counter to the saint's;
> the bon vivant and the philanthropist would trip
> each other up; the philosopher and the lady-killer
> could not well keep house in the same tenement of

clay. Such different characters may conceivably at
the outset of life be *possible* to a man. But to make
any one of them actual, the rest must more or less
be suppressed. So the seeker of his truest, strong-
est, deepest self must review the list carefully and
pick out the one on which to stake his salvation.
All other selves thereupon become unreal, but the
fortunes of this self are real. Its failures are real
failures, its triumphs real triumphs, carrying shame
and gladness with them. This is as strong an example as there is of the selective industry of the mind.
... Our thought, incessantly deciding, among
many things of a kind, which ones for it shall be
realities, here chooses one of many possible selves
or characters, and forthwith reckons it no shame to
fail in any of those not adopted expressly as its
own [Vol. 1, pp. 309-310].

Although few of us would disagree with these ideas, we characteristically fail to apply them in our lives. Again and again we
hear people say, with some finality, "I had no choice"—parents
punishing their children, bankers raising their interest rates, national leaders spending huge amounts on military weapons systems. Can it be that there are really no alternatives to the actions they have taken? Or is it, rather, that they were wearing
blinders that kept all but one possibility invisible? The first
necessity for good decision making is to remove such blinders.

It is true, of course, that possibilities, although they may
be numerous, are not unlimited. Another misleading remark we
often hear, especially in inspirational addresses to young people,
is "You can be anything you want to be." Every person's life is
hedged about by real limitations, and a part of one's task is to
identify and accept them. Each of us starts out lacking qualities
we should like to possess, and the longer we live, the more limitations we accumulate, because the choices we make require us
to rule out possibilities. Not every girl has the possibility of becoming a ballerina or an opera star, and a boy who spends all his
spare time tinkering with automobile engines can probably not

have the option some years later of becoming an outstanding surgeon, although midlife shifts of this magnitude are not so rare as they once were.

It is also true that choice may become more difficult if one faces too many possibilities. Toffler (1971) has called attention to the problem of *overchoice* that confronts modern men and women. Our communication, advertising, and marketing techniques confront us with the necessity of constantly making obvious choices about comparatively trivial matters. Which detergent? Which laxative? Which deodorant? One useful self-management policy is not to allocate too much of our scarcest resource, time, to the making of unimportant choices. It is the choices of work, spouse, religion, cause, or place to live that are worth spending time on.

Varieties of Choices

The choices one needs to make in the conduct of life are of several kinds. As has been suggested in Chapter Eight, perhaps the most fundamental is the choice of *direction*. A useful metaphor f᷉ the course of life is the concept of alternative paths or roads along which one might move. Some may be blocked, but others are open. One may take as a working assumption that for any person at any stage of life there are numerous directional possibilities, if we can only find them. The image of alternative paths is often used in connection with occupational choices, but it can be descriptive of many other life situations. A woman who is under constant stress because of her inability to find time for all the responsibilities she carries— a demanding job, a husband and two adolescent children, a large house and garden, an active social life, and a commitment to community betterment—may see only two alternatives, either to give up her career and devote her life to home and family or to arrange for a divorce or separation that will leave her free to pursue her career. A little reflection will show that there are several others. She might hire a live-in housekeeper who would relieve her of all the house and garden work. She might arrange with her employer to work half-time for the next several years.

She might analyze her social life and restrict it to specified times and only a few people. She might give up the community activity for the time being. People who manage their lives well repeatedly analyze the directions in which they are moving and consider major or minor shifts of direction to meet new circumstances.

By thinking in this way, one can often bypass rather than confront the psychological difficulties for which so many people are seeking therapy. Even serious symptoms like phobias, obsessions, or hallucinations do not always interfere with rewarding and productive lives, as the careers of so many artists, writers, and musicians testify. Take, for example, Elizabeth Barrett Browning. An account of her life before she met Robert Browning reads like a particularly upsetting chapter of a psychiatry textbook, yet all this time she was writing poetry so exquisite as to make a deep impression on him, and their marriage, which would have seemed to have everything against it, was an unusually happy one. On a more everyday level, worries a student suffers over intellectual inadequacy, inferiority feelings, and loneliness may disappear when he or she changes educational plans and starts working on something of vital interest. Years ago I wrote a paper for a counseling journal entitled "Minimum Change Therapy," recommending that counselors seek to bring about the smallest possible change in direction that would allow the client to move forward. A change of just a few degrees in direction can make a very large difference in where one is after a few months or a few years. Living creatures are not static. They are always going somewhere.

We need to choose not only among possibilities for action but also among schemata for organizing perceptions and impulses and feelings that accompany them. Because life situations are inherently ambiguous, we can assume there is usually more than one way of interpreting them. Thus, we are free to choose to interpret them in ways that help rather than hinder us in coping with life. Such an assumption underlies the cognitive therapies discussed in previous sections. The depressed, suicidal college student was able to produce a new script about his childhood that markedly changed his feelings about himself. A person can learn to search for alternative interpretations whenever depressing situations are encountered and thus exercise some control over his or her moods. As with other choices, possibilities are not unlimited. The people we meet in some situations are insulting and hostile. We do sometimes behave in ways that make others dislike and reject us. But ordinarily we can discover alternative interpretations not so overwhelmingly negative as those that occur to us first.

It is also often, if not always, true that several feelings or impulses are simultaneously present, so that one can choose which should be expressed. To do this one must cultivate *reflection*, delaying one's response until there has been time for second thoughts—and perhaps third, fourth, and fifth thoughts. Centuries before the science of psychology came into existence, sages were recommending such a delay, with maxims like "Count ten before replying." In recent times much research has compared reflective with impulsive children, demonstrating the advantages of the reflective style. Habits of reflectiveness are learned in early childhood, but a person of any age can cultivate them. Habits of waiting for second thoughts seem at first glance to be out of harmony with current emphasis on spontaneity and self-expression, but this is not necessarily true. One may choose to respond angrily to one's attacker even if one is aware of other possibilities, or one may choose to reply courteously without denying one's anger. It is beginning to be recognized that even in encounter groups, where confrontations and attacks used to be encouraged, immediate impulse needs to be tempered by reflection. Yalom (1975), after intensive studies of such groups, has reformulated some common assumptions held by participants along these lines. The first of these reformulations expresses the new trend: "Feelings, not thought" should be altered to "Feelings, only with thought."

Special importance attaches to the moral and ethical choices we make because of their effect on the lives of others besides ourselves. The codes we live by consist mainly of "Thou shalt nots" and often give us little guidance about what we *should* do. To the politician we say, "Thou shalt not accept contributions from Mafia-related businesses," but he or she still has to decide how to finance a campaign. To the researcher we say, "Thou shalt not use people as subjects without their informed consent," but he or she still has to choose a scientifically sound design for an investigation, using only subjects able and willing to give it.

We are caught in the trap of our *bipolar* thinking—good versus evil, dark versus light, friend versus foe. In order to make good moral choices in the complex world we live in, we must abandon the assumption that wrong behavior has an opposite that is necessarily right. We must recognize that in any situation there are several alternative possibilities for action, each entailing multiple consequences. At the outset we may not be able to see many of these possibilities. The first responsibility of the person making moral choices is to locate and bring to light some of these invisible alternatives. This calls for imaginative thinking about actions and their consequences. Like the ripples that spread out in all directions when a stone breaks the surface of a pond, consequences extend in all directions from actions. One can never be sure of having done the *right* thing. One can only say, "I believe I have done the *best* thing under the circumstances." At the time this is being written, the report of the commission set up to solve the Social Security problem has just been made public and its recommendations accepted by leaders of both political parties. In explaining these recommendations, the chairman of the commission made an eloquent plea for the approach being discussed here. The commission explored a number of alternatives, none of them really considered good. The ones they finally agreed on were the best of the possibilities. That is their ethical justification.

In simpler cultures and past periods of history, moral choices for most people did not involve such possibility comparisons, except perhaps for a few leaders and privileged individuals. We face them today because many more of us possess money, status, or influence. For example, the young woman of today has many more options than her pioneer grandmother had. And the manager of a multinational corporation, the diplomat trying to negotiate a treaty, and the government official attempting to deal with a depressed economy must look at a staggering array of possibilities.

One branch of psychological research is directly relevant to the matter we have been considering: the study of creative thinking. How the great creators of art, music, literature, architecture, and science differ from ordinary people has always been an intriguing problem. Since 1950 this problem has been in the forefront of research, initiated by a paper of Guilford's (1950). Many personality traits and motivational factors have been identified, but the product most useful in the present connection is the concept of *divergent* thinking, the kind that does not lead to a single right answer but to an assortment of possible answers. This is important to artists, as James' example of the sculptor and the stone, quoted earlier, suggests. But the research also has implications for ordinary people. One test frequently used asks the subject to think of as many uses as he or she can for a common object, such as a tin can, a brick, or a newspaper. Other tests call for making up stories to fit pictures, thinking of clever titles for cartoons, or elaborating simple line drawings into sketches. The sheer number of answers to the initial question provides a measure of ideational fluency, their rarity is used to assess originality, and the number of shifts from one category to another measures flexibility. One research design that became quite popular compared two groups of children, the first consisting of children who scored high on tests of "creativity" and average or below on IQ, the second consisting of children who scored high on IQ but average or below on the "creativity" tests (Getzels and Jackson, 1962). Some interesting differences turned up. Children gifted in divergent thinking were less interested than the others in success, more interested in creative expression. Their stories were marked by fantasy, more humor, more violence, and more obscenity. Their teachers found them less docile, more troublesome than the others. It is too early to conclude that such children are the creators of tomorrow, but the findings have suggested such a hypothesis.

What is more important for our purposes is the finding that even ordinary people can and do deal actively with possibilities, recognizing, selecting, combining, and reorganizing. Furthermore, research suggests that divergent thinking can be stimulated and facilitated in children and in adults. Some teachers have been able to raise the level of performance in their classrooms (Torrance, 1963). In business and industry a great many procedures have proved their worth in increasing the number of diverse and innovative ideas that workers generate (Stein, 1974, 1975). Brainstorming is a procedure in which individuals in a group concentrate on producing as many ideas as possible, regardless of how fantastic or silly they seem. A little book by Adams (1974) analyzes for those who use the procedure the kinds of blocks that obstruct the brainstorming process and suggests some practical methods of "blockbusting." I referred earlier to the work of Shure and Spivack (1978), who have trained children to see multiple possibilities in interpersonal situations that call for decisions and actions. What all these training procedures attempt to accomplish is the overcoming of unnecessary self-imposed restrictions. If the task, for example, is to list possible uses for a tin can, one tends to assume that it must be left in its present shape. Unless one realizes that this restriction is unnecessary, one is likely to get a low score for fluency and extremely low scores for originality and flexibility because the only uses one thinks of will be for a container. Once one gets rid of the restriction, dozens of possibilities appear. Cut the can open, flatten it out, melt it, cut it in strips, sharpen the edges, paint it, punch holes in it, and dozens of new uses can be listed.

Setting Priorities

Maintaining control over one's own life requires not only seeing possibilities and making choices but also arranging the things one has chosen in priority order. Because one's time is limited, it is not enough to make single choices one at a time. The commitments they involve can lead to troublesome problems. Setting priorities is often difficult, and there has been little or no psychological study of the process. Some of the difficulty arises from the fact that our culture and the learning opportunities it provides do not encourage us to make several choices at a time. For example, on a national scale, the huge government deficits that are the number one concern of Americans at the time this is being written are partly the result of the standard parliamentary procedures Congress and other organized bodies use. Congress votes on appropriations bills one by one, and if the programs such bills authorize are good ones, especially if they are popular with the citizens, they are likely to pass. There is no established place in the system for *ordering* major budget items from most to least important. Similarly, people with good credit ratings run up huge totals of indebtedness because they lack experience or training in arranging in priority order the wants that determine purchases. Each purchase may be a good one satisfying a real need, but their total can produce a catastrophic financial problem.

Priorities like the foregoing are based on the relative importance of items. Others have to do with time. "What should be done first, second, third, or later?" This kind of thinking is often important in career plans, as counselors have pointed out. A freshman student may decide that what he most wants to do with his life is to practice medicine. The income, the prestige, and the opportunities for human service are factors that weigh heavily in favor of this choice. But it is advisable for him to consider second and perhaps third choices. If he finds at the end of his first college year that he has made only Ds in chemistry and physics and dislikes biology intensely, it is likely that the ordering of the three possibilities will change. Or if he finishes a premedical program with a respectable record but finds himself extremely reluctant to face the prospect of four years of grueling work in medical school, his second choice, banking, may look much more attractive than it did when he entered college. It is a real advantage to have several strings for one's bow.

In an earlier chapter I discussed Simon's (1981) concept of satisficing rather than maximizing. Arising from research on computer problem solving, this concept means that the search for solutions stops as soon as an alternative turns up that meets predetermined criteria. Applied to the process of life planning, it calls for ending the exploration of possibilities as soon as one (or a few, if one is ordering priorities) comes to light that meets one's personal criteria for the good life, accepting the limitations that go with the choice. The importance of exploration of possibilities is a major theme of this book. The satisficing principle makes such exploration manageable. One need not spend large amounts of one's limited time looking for the *best* doctor to perform an operation, the *most* prestigious college, the *perfect* place to live.

The Role of Chance

Bandura (1982b) has called attention to the large part chance plays in setting life directions. A chance meeting, a visit to someone's home, a book taken almost at random from a library shelf—on such happenings the course of life often depends. One striking example Bandura gives is that of a young man named Paul Watkins, who as a talented teenager seemed to be headed for a constructive and rewarding life. An attempt to visit a friend who he found no longer lived at his former residence brought him into contact with the Manson "family," who now lived there, in the days before they became notorious. He became entangled in their affairs, attracted by the pleasures of communal love and drugs, and thus embarked on a course of life that almost ruined him and required years to turn around. Other chance happenings Bandura relates have beneficial rather than harmful effects. Nancy Reagan, for example, met her future husband because she happened to have received in the mail Communist material intended for another person with the same name, and her concern that she might be considered a Communist sympathizer led her to seek advice from Ronald Reagan, then president of the Screen Actors Guild. Each of us could probably supply from our own experience other examples of such fortuitous events.

If one wishes to plan and control one's own life, one must be prepared to take advantage of chance events and consider them in the light of the thinking one has done about values and directions. Chance can provide raw material for choice. And choice is the essential process in directing and controlling one's own life.

Summary

The basic ideas that a given situation has more than one possible outcome and that one's own choice can determine which of these is actualized are especially useful in self-management.

In applying these ideas one needs to analyze one's situation, searching actively for alternative interpretations of it and alternative responses to it. This involves identifying preconceptions that can blind one to some of the alternatives. Limiting factors in oneself and one's circumstances must be taken into consideration, but with the realization that they may not all be as restrictive as one at first assumes. Once alternative courses of action are recognized, it is then important to think ahead about possible consequences of each.

The objective of such thinking is the making of enlightened choices. These are of many varieties besides the obvious ones of careers, spouses, and the like. We may choose the organizing schemata we employ, the directions our lives take, the life-styles we adopt, and many other things.

The components one chooses for one's life cannot just be added together or laid end to end. The task remains of fitting them together into an organized whole. It involves setting priorities and considering second and third as well as first choices.

The knowledge about human life that psychologists have accumulated, as well as the insights attained by thinkers down through the ages, constitutes a storehouse of possibilities from which one can draw in designing and managing one's own life.

CHAPTER 11

Implications for Psychology
and Psychologists

❖ ❖ ❖ ❖ ❖ ❖ ❖ ❖ ❖ ❖ ❖ ❖

Probability and Possibility

Although the fact has not usually been emphasized or even recognized, the concept of multiple possibilities is built into the very foundation of scientific psychology. Probability theory has played a very large part in the development of the science. Once curious mathematicians discovered that there was order in the way chance events distributed themselves, the way was open for the investigation of phenomena never before considered amenable to scientific study. The bell-shaped normal curve proved enormously useful. It made it possible, in areas where exact predictions were impossible, to make *statistical* predictions and to estimate the amount of error they might involve. Techniques of measurement based on the normal curve were used to quantify psychological performances and processes so that different people, different situations, and different procedures could be compared. By combining two separate normal distributions, one could determine the extent to which two variables were related. If one wished to prove that an experimental treatment was effective, one could compare the results the treatment had produced with the theoretical "chance" distribution that presumably would have been obtained without any special treatment. Work in these and many other directions branched off from the main trunk of probability theory. The normal curve can be viewed as the curve of multiple possibilities.

Although psychologists and other social scientists use the term *chance* constantly, they are not very explicit about what they mean by it. If pressed for an explanation, most psychologists would probably say that it stands for the totality of the effects of numerous unanalyzed or unanalyzable causes. Because it is not possible to identify and measure all these variables, one must be content with statistical rather than exact predictions, but the same assumption of complete determinism underlies both.

This, however, is not the only way in which *chance* can be interpreted. Many years ago, the unappreciated philosopher C. S. Peirce (1892/1958) proposed that *chance* could refer to a genuine multiplicity of possible outcomes of any situation. Thus, the event that actually occurs is inherently *un*predictable. According to this view, the laws of nature are not absolutely ironclad. There is some "play" in the system, room for spontaneity, unprecedented happenings limited and regulated but not absolutely determined by what went before. "By thus admitting pure spontaneity . . . as a character of the universe, acting always and everywhere though restrained within narrow bounds by law, producing infinitesimal departures from law continually, and great ones with infinite infrequency, I account for all the variety and diversity of the universe" (p. 175).

There is a core of uncertainty at the center of things. Physicists who work in the realm of the microscopic have long ago accepted this assumption. The biologist Monod (1971) has written a profound essay dealing with its implications for the life sciences. The whole biosphere, according to Monod, is a unique occurrence not predictable from other occurrences: "The thesis I shall present in this book is that the biosphere does not contain a predictable class of objects or of events but constitutes a particular occurrence, compatible indeed with first principles, but not *deducible* from those principles and therefore essentially unpredictable. . . . Among all the occurrences possible in the universe the a priori probability of any one of them verges upon zero. Yet the universe exists; particular events must take place in it, the probability of which (before the event) was infinitesimal" (pp. 43, 145).

This is the essence of the message the present book has attempted to communicate, leading to a replacement of the assumption of *absolute* determinism by one of *limited* determinism. Accepting the hypothesis that a situation may have several possible outcomes, that a cause or set of causes may have several possible effects, and that an action may be traced to one of several possible causes does not mean that lawfulness has been banished from the universe or that *anything* may happen. The body of knowledge accumulated under the assumption of strict determinism still stands. Stimuli that we present, controls that we impose do *affect* behavior even if they do not determine it. We can continue to improve our understanding of human nature even if we give up attempts to predict and control it.

Part Two of the book traced the progress of research on perception, cognition, learning, social phenomena, and development, with examples of ways in which the concept of multiple possibilities was related to that progress. From the beginning research psychologists encountered multiplicity and diversity difficult to reconcile with the kind of psychological science they were trying to build. One way they hit on to deal with variability was to apply the physicists' concept of "error" to the measurements they made and to use the statistical techniques available for quantifying error. As long as they were dealing with simpler aspects of human nature like sensory processes or memory for digits, this maneuver worked well because the distributions they obtained from groups of subjects or sequences of trials conformed to the normal curve and were narrow in scope, most of the measurements clustered closely around a central value. Diversity could be ignored and the standard deviation of the distribution regarded as an indicator of the "chance" error connected with the "true" figure.

The complex structure of inferential statistics rests on this foundation. The research approach considered most meaningful, the experiment, in its simplest form involves comparison of a group of subjects undergoing some special treatment, the "experimental" group, with a similarly selected group left untreated, the "control" group. Suppose that the average of the scores for the experimental group turns out to be higher than the average for the control group? How can the experimenter be certain that the difference is greater than the difference chance alone might have produced? Unless this can be demonstrated, no firm conclusion can be drawn. The challenge was met by assuming that the chance differences themselves were distributed normally, with an average of zero. This is the *null hypothesis,* the basis for the conclusions in hundreds, perhaps thousands, of experiments. Empirical tests indicated that chance differences did indeed distribute themselves normally, and statisticians were able to work out ways of estimating the parameters of this chance distribution from variability data the experiment produced. The phrase "significant at the 5 percent level" means that out of 100 comparisons of groups selected randomly from the same population, not more than 5 would produce as large a difference as the experiment showed.

As psychological research moved into more complex areas, from sensation to perception to cognition—from memory for nonsense syllables to memory for stories and explanatory passages, for example—the assumption that all the nonchance variability could be attributed to the experimental treatment came to seem less tenable. In experiments on complex processes both the variability from trial to trial and the individual differences within experimental and control groups often turn out to be large. Is it right to lump them together as chance error? Attempts were made to identify other sources of differences between individuals and between groups in addition to the experimental treatment factor. Multivariate techniques and more discriminating significance tests became available, complexities it is not necessary to go into here.

But as cognitive psychology and ecological psychology gained ground, it has appeared less and less feasible to design experiments in which all of the variability can be accounted for by what the experimenter did to or told the subjects, by other identifiable factors such as age, sex, and socioeconomic status, and by chance error. Take, for example, an experiment designed to find out whether a new method of teaching the multiplication table works better than the one a school has been using. With throws of a coin or tables of random numbers, third-grade children are assigned to experimental and control groups. Then what happens? If they meet in separate rooms and are taught by different teachers, the finding that Group A has learned significantly more than Group B may mean only that Teacher A is more competent than Teacher B. The difference between teachers can hardly be considered a chance difference. If, to control it, the two groups are taught at different times by the same teacher, A's superiority may arise from the fact that some hours of the day are more favorable than others for study. If, to control this, the times at which lessons occur are randomized for both groups, there is still the possibility that the teacher's preference for the new technique and his or her desire to see the experiment succeed may have been an important factor. Questions of this sort turn out to be even more troublesome when the difference between groups turns out to be *non*significant. We cannot conclude that the experimental technique had no effect. Questions about whether all the sources of possible variation lumped together as "chance" really belong in the chance distribution have made it difficult, if not impossible, to obtain definitive results from experiments of this sort by the use of techniques that worked reasonably well in studies of simple perceptual and learning processes. It seems more useful to think of all possible influences on behavior and study it as an organized system than to try to establish the validity of a particular causal sequence. But methods of doing research on systems are far less well developed than methods for dealing with single variables.

Looking back into history, we can see that there is another way in which scientific psychology has dealt with the problem of differences from person to person and from trial to trial. This was to separate the river of research into two separate streams, one for basic processes and the other for individual differences. Quite early in the history of the new psychological laboratories, some researchers became more interested in the differences between individual scores revealed by the distributions than in what the central tendencies of the distributions were. In fact, interest in individual differences antedated by several decades the establishment of the psychological laboratories themselves. An astronomer, Bessel, looking over records of the Greenwich Observatory, was intrigued by an entry indicating that a young assistant had been dismissed because he continually reported the time of the apparent transit of a star across the hairline of a telescope nearly a second later than his master did. Bessel began trying out his fellow astronomers, measuring their exact times, and found that there was considerable variation. He called this the "personal equation." After systematic psychological research began, the *reaction time* experiment occupied an important place in the new laboratories.

Normal-curve thinking was as fundamental to the research on individual differences as it was to the research on basic processes. But the concept of what the normal distribution means was not related to chance error but, rather, to a discovery made by a Belgian mathematician, Quetelet, that all sorts of human measurements, such as height, girth, and head size, were distributed normally. Psychologists could use the curve to describe variability in many mental characteristics and to construct norm tables and derived score systems for mental tests.

Research for psychologists studying individual differences mainly took the form of attempts to find out what they were related to. The *correlation coefficient,* another by-product of normal-curve thinking, was the statistical technique most often used. Such coefficients indicated both the direction and the magnitude of the relation between two measured characteristics. A vast structure of methodology was built on the foundation of the correlation coefficient—regression, factor analysis, and many other ways of processing data.

Thus, scientific psychology very early was split into the two disciplines Cronbach analyzed in 1957. Many others besides Cronbach have pointed out the unfortunate effects of this division. Experimental psychologists draw conclusions from their findings and base predictions on these conclusions without taking into account the diversity of individual responses to the stimulating situation. Correlational psychologists generate elaborate theories about psychological traits such as intelligence without taking into consideration what experiments have shown about mental processes underlying these traits. After decades of argument psychologists still cannot agree on whether there really is such an entity as general intelligence, although dozens of tests for it have been constructed, and dozens of correlational studies have produced evidence that the scores are at least moderately related to many other measured characteristics. Broader horizons for psychologists in both fields are perhaps in sight.

Systems and Structures

In previous chapters there has been considerable emphasis on the importance of thinking in terms of interactive systems rather than single variables. Fundamental to systems thinking is the concept of *structure*. In the example of the experiment on the teaching of arithmetic used in the previous section, mental structures in the teacher and in the individual pupils affect the results, structures that are invisible and not manipulable for research purposes. The term *structure* is somewhat ambiguous; it connotes solidity that psychological structures do not have. I have defined the term as "a system of self-regulating transformations, never observed directly but inferred from its effects" (Tyler, 1978a, p. 109). Piaget (1970), in his book on structuralism, puts it this way: "The notion of structure is comprised of three key ideas: the idea of wholeness, the idea of transformation, and the idea of self-regulation" (p. 5). Hypotheses about causal sequences and about independent and dependent variables are replaced by hypotheses about the transformation of structures.

In research on cognitive processes, special terms for particular kinds of structures have appeared. *Schema* can be defined as "a cognitive structure that represents some stimulus domain" (Taylor and Crocker, 1981, p. 123). It includes the attributes of the domain, ways of gathering further information about it, and motivation to apply it in new situations. For example, a woman may have a food schema built around distinctions between junk foods and nutritious foods, caloric value, and freedom from chemical additives. It exercises some control over what she eats, what she buys, and what she reads in magazines and newspapers. Anderson (1980, p. 128) defines *schemata* as "large, complex units of knowledge that organize much of what we know about general categories of objects, classes of events, and types of people."

A term that designates a particular kind of schema is *script*. This consists of an organization of a sequence of events into a narrative. Incorporated in its structure are feelings and motivations along with cognitive meanings. The mental structure controlling most of our behavior in frequently encountered situations such as a restaurant, an airplane trip, or a concert is a script. We also make use of scripts to organize our memories of our own past lives. Such narrative schemata are also called *scenarios*.

Another term frequently encountered in discussions of the cognitive structures underlying behavior is *strategy*. It is used in explaining how memories are stored and retrieved and how the heuristic search process in problem solving occurs. Strategies have an action connotation that is not necessarily involved in other kinds of structure. They are not just ways of representing the world but plans for dealing with it. For example, "chunking" and "rehearsal" are common memorizing strategies.

In thinking about all these varieties of mental structure, we need to make a place for another concept not so frequently met with in the discussions, the concept of *repertoire*. In all the many learning situations one encounters, it seems likely that several schemata for organizing some kinds of knowledge would develop, several alternative scripts for some situations and sequences of happenings, several problem-solving strategies. One of the alternatives may predominate over the others, or they may all function at one time or another. In research or in the management of one's practical affairs, it is an advantage to have such a repertoire from which to choose.

The diversity and flexibility that comes from the possession of repertoires of cognitive structures is one meaning of *creativity*. Mainstream psychology, with its goal of predicting and controlling behavior, has never known just what to do with research on creativity. The more creative a person is, the harder he or she is to predict with any precision. And if what is created were predictable, it could no longer be described as creative. Some acceptance of the idea of multiple possibilities is essential if the creative process is to be understood. It involves awareness of alternatives, evaluation of possible consequences, shifts from one plan to another. Not only artists but also ordinary people who come up with novel solutions to problems think in this way.

The concept of multiple possibilities is basic to both probability theory and general systems theory, for the same reason. This is that from four units on up, there are always more possible combinations of units in any aggregation than units themselves. This fact is at the very heart of the mathematics of probability. For example, if we have three units, A, B, and C, there are three possible combinations, AB, AC, and BC. But for four units there are six combinations, and for ten units forty-five combinations, considering only pairs. If we think of larger sets, the number becomes even greater. For 100 units, there are 4,950 two-unit combinations and 323,400 three-unit combinations.

Turning to systems theory, we realize that a system is by definition a combination of units and that there are always many possible ways of putting together an organized whole. Simon (1981), whose recommendations for a science of design I have discussed in some detail in Chapter Five, emphasizes this fact in his chapter "The Architecture of Complexity" (pp. 193–229). A system is a hierarchy of subsystems and is to some extent decomposable into these. Combining subsystems in various ways produces various evolutionary species, various personalities, various cultures.

What makes multiple possibility thinking especially important for humanity is the place it makes for *choice*. A small fraction of the available possibilities are constantly being selected to be actualized. Selection occurs in the long march of evolution, the functioning of living systems from the simplest to the most complex, and the development of individuals and societies. Human beings can accomplish this selection through conscious choice. As Peirce pointed out, it is what we call chance that makes choice possible. Because there are alternative possibilities, there will always be diversity in personalities, cultures, institutions, and ways of solving human problems. We cannot hope to reach full agreement on political systems, moral codes, or designs for living, but we can consider the alternatives from which choices can be made and discard unpromising possibilities. The challenge to psychology is to face the full panoply of complex reality and organize it in ways that make sense. The challenge to the people psychology serves is to choose the kinds of organization that are most useful for them in planning and conducting their lives.

REFERENCES

Adams, J. L. *Conceptual Blockbusting.* Stanford, Calif.: Stanford Alumni Association, 1974.

Adorno, T. W., and others. *The Authoritarian Personality.* New York: Harper & Row, 1950.

Ajzen, I., and Fishbein, M. "Attitude-Behavior Relations: A Theoretical Analysis and Review of Empirical Research." *Psychological Bulletin,* 1977, *84,* 888–918.

Allport, F. H. *Social Psychology.* Boston: Houghton Mifflin, 1924.

Anderson, J. R. *Cognitive Psychology and Its Implications.* San Francisco: W. H. Freeman, 1980.

Anderson, J. R. (Ed.). *Cognitive Skills and Their Acquisition.* Hillsdale, N.J.: Erlbaum, 1981.

Atkinson, R. C., and Shiffrin, R. M. "Human Memory: A Proposed System and Its Control Processes." In K. W. Spence and J. T. Spence (Eds.), *The Psychology of Learning and Motivation.* Vol. 2. New York: Academic Press, 1968.

Baldwin, J. M. *Mental Development in the Child and the Race.* New York: Macmillan, 1894.

Baltes, P. B., Reese, H. W., and Lipsitt, L. P. "Life-Span Developmental Psychology." *Annual Review of Psychology,* 1980, *31,* 65–110.

Bandura, A. "Self-Efficacy Mechanism in Human Agency."
    American Psychologist, 1982a, *37,* 122-147.
Bandura, A. "The Psychology of Chance Encounters and Life
    Paths." *American Psychologist,* 1982b, *37,* 747-755.
Barker, R. G., and Associates. *Habitats, Environments, and Hu-*
    man Behavior: Studies in Ecological Psychology and Eco-
    Behavioral Science. San Francisco: Jossey-Bass, 1978.
Barker, R. G., and Wright, H. F. *One Boy's Day.* New York:
    Harper & Row, 1951.
Bartlett, F. C. *Remembering: A Study in Experimental and So-*
    cial Psychology. Cambridge: Cambridge University Press,
    1932.
Bem, D. J. "Self-Perception Theory." *Advances in Experimental*
    Social Psychology, 1972, *6,* 1-62.
Berlyne, D. E. "Curiosity and Exploration." *Science,* 1966,
    153, 25-33.
Berry, J. W. *Human Ecology and Cognitive Styles.* New York:
    Wiley, 1976.
Bertalanffy, L. von. *General Systems Theory.* New York: Brazil-
    lier, 1968.
Binet, A., and Simon, T. "Methodes Nouvelles pour le Diagnos-
    tic du Niveau Intellectual des Abnormaux" [New Methods
    for the Diagnosis of Intellectual Level of Abnormals]. *L'An-*
    nee Psycologique, 1905, *11,* 191-244.
Block, J. "Assimilation, Accommodation, and the Dynamics of
    Personality Development." *Child Development,* 1982, *53,*
    281-295.
Broadbent, D. E. *Perception and Communication.* Oxford,
    England: Pergamon Press, 1958.
Bruner, J., Oliver, R., and Greenfield, P. *Studies in Growth.*
    New York: Wiley, 1966.
Bryan, W. L., and Harter, N. "Studies on the Telegraphic Lan-
    guages: The Acquisition of a Hierarchy of Habits." *Psycho-*
    logical Review, 1899, *6,* 345-375.
Bullock, D. "On the Current and Potential Scope of Generative
    Theories of Cognitive Development." In K. W. Fischer (Ed.),
    New Directions for Child Development: Cognitive Develop-
    ment, no. 12. San Francisco: Jossey-Bass, 1981.

Cairns, R. B. *Social Development: The Origins and Plasticity of Interchanges.* San Francisco: W. H. Freeman, 1979.

Cairns, R. B., and Ornstein, P. A. "Developmental Psychology." In E. Hearst (Ed.), *The First Century of Experimental Psychology.* New York: Wiley, 1979.

Calvert, R., Jr., and Draves, W. A. *Free Universities and Learning Referral Centers.* Washington, D.C.: National Center for Educational Statistics, 1978.

Campbell, J. (Ed.). *The Portable Jung.* New York: Viking, 1971.

Chandler, M., and Boyes, M. "Social Cognitive Development." In B. B. Wolman (Ed.), *Handbook of Developmental Psychology.* Englewood Cliffs, N.J.: Prentice-Hall, 1982.

Chase, W. G., and Ericsson, K. A. "Skilled Memory." In J. R. Anderson (Ed.), *Cognitive Skills and Their Acquisition.* Hillsdale, N.J.: Erlbaum, 1981.

Chase, W. G., and Simon, H. A. "The Mind's Eye in Chess." In W. G. Chase (Ed.), *Visual Information Processing.* New York: Academic Press, 1973.

Cialdini, R. B., Petty, R. E., and Cacioppo, J. T. "Attitude and Attitude Change." *Annual Review of Psychology,* 1981, *32,* 357-404.

Collingwood, R. G. *Essays in the Philosophy of History.* New York: McGraw-Hill, 1965.

Collins, A. M., and Quillian, M. R. "Retrieval Time from Semantic Memory." *Journal of Verbal Learning and Verbal Behavior,* 1969, *8,* 240-247.

Corcoran, D. W. J., and Jackson, A. "Basic Processes and Strategies in Visual Search." In S. Dornic (Ed.), *Attention and Performance.* Hillsdale, N.J.: Erlbaum, 1977.

Cronbach, H. J. "The Two Disciplines of Scientific Psychology." *American Psychologist,* 1957, *12,* 671-684.

Danto, A. C. *Analytical Philosophy of History.* Cambridge: Cambridge University Press, 1965.

Darwin, C. *On the Origin of Species.* London: J. Murray, 1859.

Davidson, D. "The Material Mind." In J. Haugeland (Ed.), *Mind Design.* Cambridge, Mass.: M.I.T. Press, 1981.

Dember, M., and Warm, S. *Psychology of Perception.* New York: Holt, Rinehart and Winston, 1979.

Dennett, D. C. "Intentional Systems." In J. Haugeland (Ed.), *Mind Design*. Cambridge, Mass.: M.I.T. Press, 1981.

Dickinson, A., and Mackintosh, N. J. "Classical Conditioning in Animals." *Annual Review of Psychology*, 1978, *29*, 587–612.

Donders, F. C. "On the Speed of Mental Processes." *Acta Psychologica*, 1969, *30*, 412–431. (Originally published 1868.)

Eagly, A. H., and Himmelfarb, S. "Attitudes and Opinions." *Annual Review of Psychology*, 1978, *29*, 517–554.

Ebbinghaus, H. *Über das Gedachtnis: Untersuchen zur experimentellen psychologie* [On Memory: Investigations in Experimental Psychology]. New York: Dover, 1964. (Originally published 1885.)

Ellis, A. *Reason and Emotion in Psychotherapy*. New York: Lyle Stuart, 1962.

Erikson, E. H. *Childhood and Society*. (2nd ed.) New York: Norton, 1963.

Eysenck, H. J. "The Effects of Psychotherapy: An Evaluation." *Journal of Consulting Psychology*, 1952, *16*, 319–324.

Festinger, L. *A Theory of Cognitive Dissonance*. New York: Harper & Row, 1957.

Fischer, K. W. "A Theory of Cognitive Development: The Control and Construction of Hierarchies of Skills." *Psychological Review*, 1980, *87*, 477–531.

Fishbein, M., and Ajzen, I. *Belief, Attitude, Intention, and Behavior: An Introduction to Theory and Research*. Reading, Mass.: Addison-Wesley, 1975.

Fitts, P. M., and Posner, M. I. *Human Performance*. Monterey, Calif.: Brooks/Cole, 1967.

Flavell, J. H. "On Cognitive Development." *Child Development*, 1982, *53*, 1–10.

Garcia, J., Ervin, F. R., and Koelling, R. A. "Learning with Prolonged Delay of Reinforcement." *Psychonomic Science*, 1966, *5*, 121–122.

Getzels, J. W., and Jackson, P. W. *Creativity and Intelligence*. New York: Wiley, 1962.

Gibson, J. J. *The Ecological Approach to Visual Perception*. Boston: Houghton Mifflin, 1979.

Goldfarb, W. "Effects of Early Institutional Care on Adolescent

Personality." *Journal of Experimental Education,* 1943, *12,* 106-129.

Goldfarb, W. "Effects of Early Institutional Care on Adolescent Personality: Rorschach Data." *American Journal of Orthopsychiatry,* 1944, *14,* 441-447.

Goldstein, A. P. "Relationship Enhancement Methods." In F. H. Kanfer and A. P. Goldstein (Eds.), *Helping People Change.* Elmsford, N.Y.: Pergamon Press, 1975.

Goldstein, K. M., and Blackman, S. *Cognitive Style.* New York: Wiley, 1978.

Gottesman, I. I. "Developmental Genetics and Ontogenetic Psychology: Overdue Detente and Propositions from a Matchmaker." In A. D. Peck (Ed.), *Minnesota Symposium on Child Psychology.* Vol. 8. Minneapolis: University of Minnesota Press, 1974.

Gould, J. "The Evolutionary Biology of Constraint." *Daedalus,* 1980, *109*(2), 39-52.

Guilford, J. P. "Creativity." *American Psychologist,* 1950, *14,* 469-479.

Hall, G. S. *Adolescence: Its Psychology and its Relations to Physiology, Anthropology, Sociology, Sex, Crime, Religion, and Education.* (2 vols.) New York: Appleton, 1904.

Haugeland, J. (Ed.). *Mind Design.* Cambridge, Mass.: M.I.T. Press, 1981.

Heider, F. "Attitudes and Cognitive Organization." *Journal of Psychology,* 1946, *21,* 107-112.

Higgins, E. T., Herman, C. P., and Zanna, M. P. *Social Cognition: The Ontario Symposium.* Vol. 1. Hillsdale, N.J.: Erlbaum, 1981.

Hilgard, E. R. "Consciousness in Contemporary Psychology." *Annual Review of Psychology,* 1980, *31,* 1-26.

Hochberg, J. *Perception.* (2nd ed.) Englewood Cliffs, N.J.: Prentice-Hall, 1978.

Hovland, C. I., Lumsdaine, A. A., and Sheffield, F. D. *Experiments in Mass Communication.* Princeton, N.J.: Princeton University Press, 1949.

Hull, C. L. *Principles of Behavior.* New York: Appleton-Century-Crofts, 1943.

Hunt, E. B., Davidson, J., and Lansman, M. "Individual Differences in Long-Term Memory Access." *Memory and Cognition,* 1981, *9,* 599–608.

Hunt, E. B., and Lansman, M. "Cognitive Theory Applied to Individual Differences." In N. K. Estes (Ed.), *Handbook of Learning and Cognitive Processes.* Vol. 1. Hillsdale, N.J.: Erlbaum, 1975.

Hunt, J. McV. *Intelligence and Experience.* New York: Ronald Press, 1961.

Hunt, J. McV. "Psychological Development and the Educational Enterprise." *Educational Theory,* 1975, *25,* 333–353.

Hunt, J. McV. "Psychological Development: Early Experience." *Annual Review of Psychology,* 1979, *30,* 103–143.

Hurvich, L. M. *Color Vision.* Sunderland, Mass.: Sinauer Associates, 1981.

James, W. *The Principles of Psychology.* New York: Holt, 1890.

Jantsch, E. *The Self-Organizing Universe.* Elmsford, N.Y.: Pergamon Press, 1980.

Jaynes, J. *The Origins of Consciousness in the Breakdown of the Bicameral Mind.* Boston: Houghton Mifflin, 1976.

Jensen, A. R. "Chronometric Analysis of Intelligence." *Journal of Social and Biological Structure,* 1980, *3,* 103–122.

Jones, E. E., and Nisbett, R. E. "The Actor and the Observer: Divergent Perceptions of the Causes of Behavior." In E. E. Jones and others (Eds.), *Attribution: Perceiving the Causes of Behavior.* Morristown, N.J.: General Learning Press, 1972.

Jung, C. G. *Man and His Symbols.* New York: Doubleday, 1964.

Kahneman, D. *Attention and Effort.* Englewood Cliffs, N.J.: Prentice-Hall, 1973.

Kamin, L. J. "Predictability, Surprise, Attention, and Conditioning." In B. Campbell and R. Church (Eds.), *Punishment and Aversive Behavior.* New York: Appleton-Century-Crofts, 1969.

Kanfer, F. H., and Goldstein, A. P. *Helping People Change.* Elmsford, N.Y.: Pergamon Press, 1975.

Kelley, H. H. "Attribution Theory in Social Psychology." *Nebraska Symposium on Motivation,* 1967, *15,* 192–238.

Kelley, H. H., and Michela, J. L. "Attribution Theory and Research." *Annual Review of Psychology,* 1980, *31,* 457–501.

Klein, G. S., and Schlesinger, H. J. "Where Is the Perceiver in Perceptual Theory?" *Journal of Personality*, 1949, *18*, 32–47.

Kohlberg, L. "Moral Stages and Moralization: The Cognitive-Developmental Approach." In T. Lickona (Ed.), *Moral Development and Behavior*. New York: Holt, Rinehart and Winston, 1976.

Kuhn, T. *The Structure of Scientific Revolutions*. Chicago: University of Chicago Press, 1962.

Kuhn, T. *The Essential Tension*. Chicago: University of Chicago Press, 1977.

Langley, P., and Simon, H. A. "The Central Role of Learning in Cognition." In J. R. Anderson (Ed.), *Cognitive Skills and Their Acquisition*. Hillsdale, N.J.: Erlbaum, 1981.

Lefcourt, H. M. *Locus of Control*. Hillsdale, N.J.: Erlbaum, 1976.

LeShan, L., and Margenau, H. *Einstein's Space and Van Gogh's Sky*. New York: Macmillan, 1982.

Lewin, K. "Group Decision and Social Change." In T. M. Newcomb and E. L. Hartley (Eds.), *Readings in Social Psychology*. New York: Holt, Rinehart and Winston, 1947.

Lieberman, J. "The Romantic Rationalist." *New York Review of Books*, Dec. 2, 1982, pp. 51, 57.

Loux, M. J. (Ed.). *The Possible and the Actual*. Ithaca, N.Y.: Cornell University Press, 1979.

Lovejoy, A. O. *The Great Chain of Being*. Cambridge, Mass.: Harvard University Press, 1936.

McDougall, W. *An Introduction to Social Psychology*. London: Methuen, 1908.

Manicas, P. T., and Secord, P. F. "Implications for Psychology of the New Philosophy of Science." *American Psychologist*, 1983, *38*, 399–413.

Mayr, E. *Evolution and the Diversity of Life*. Cambridge, Mass.: Harvard University Press, 1976.

Miller, G. "Psychology as a Means of Promoting Human Welfare." *American Psychologist*, 1969, *24*, 1063–1075.

Miller, J. G. *Living Systems*. New York: McGraw-Hill, 1978.

Monod, J. *Chance and Necessity*. New York: Vintage, 1971.

Mook, D. G. "In Defense of External Invalidity." *American Psychologist*, 1983, *38*, 379–387.

Mowrer, O. H. "On the Dual Nature of Learning—A Reinterpretation of 'Conditioning' and 'Problem Solving.'" *Harvard Educational Review,* 1947, *17,* 102-148.

Newell, A., Shaw, J. C., and Simon, H. A. "Elements of a Theory of Human Problem Solving." *Psychological Review,* 1958, *65,* 151-166.

Newell, A., and Simon, H. A. "Computer Science as Empirical Inquiry: Symbols and Search." In J. Haugeland (Ed.), *Mind Design.* Cambridge, Mass.: M.I.T. Press, 1981.

Paris, S. G., and Lindauer, B. K. "The Development of Cognitive Skills During Childhood." In B. B. Wolman (Ed.), *Handbook of Developmental Psychology.* Englewood Cliffs, N.J.: Prentice-Hall, 1982.

Peirce, C. S. *Values in a Universe of Chance.* New York: Doubleday, 1958. (Originally published 1892.)

Piaget, J. *Structuralism.* New York: Basic Books, 1970.

Pick, H. L., Jr., and Saltzman, E. (Eds.). *Modes of Perceiving and Processing Information.* Hillsdale, N.J.: Erlbaum, 1978.

Popper, K. R. *Objective Knowledge.* Oxford: Oxford University Press, 1972.

Popper, K. R., and Eccles, J. C. *The Self and Its Brain.* New York: Springer, 1977.

Posner, M. I., and McLeod, P. "Information Processing Models— in Search of Elementary Operations." *Annual Review of Psychology,* 1982, *33,* 477-514.

Posner, M. I., and Shulman, G. L. "Cognitive Science." In E. Hearst (Ed.), *The First Century of Experimental Psychology.* Hillsdale, N.J.: Erlbaum, 1979.

Pressey, S. L. "Educational Acceleration." *Ohio State University Bureau of Educational Research Monographs,* 1949, *56,* 159-205.

Preyer, W. *Die Seele des Kinds.* Leipzig: Fernan, 1882. Also published as *The Mind of the Child.* (2 vols.) New York: Appleton, 1888-1889.

Prigogine, I. *From Being to Becoming.* San Francisco: W. H. Freeman, 1980.

Reason, P., and Rowan, J. (Eds.). *Human Inquiry.* New York: Wiley, 1981.

Rescher, N. *A Theory of Possibility*. Pittsburgh: University of Pittsburgh Press, 1975.

Rescorla, R. A. *Second-Order Conditioning*. Hillsdale, N.J.: Erlbaum, 1980.

Rescorla, R. A., and Holland, P. C. "Behavioral Studies of Associative Learning in Animals." *Annual Review of Psychology*, 1982, *33*, 265-308.

Resnick, L. (Ed.). *The Nature of Intelligence*. Hillsdale, N.J.: Erlbaum, 1976.

Rogers, C. R. *Counseling and Psychotherapy*. Boston: Houghton Mifflin, 1942.

Rogers, C. R. *Client-Centered Therapy*. Boston: Houghton Mifflin, 1951.

Rogers, C. R. "The Necessary and Sufficient Conditions of Therapeutic Personality Change." *Journal of Consulting Psychology*, 1957, *21*, 95-103.

Rogers, C. R. (Ed.). *The Therapeutic Relationship and Its Impact: A Study of Psychotherapy with Schizophrenics*. Madison: University of Wisconsin Press, 1967.

Rogers, C. R. *A Way of Being*. Boston: Houghton Mifflin, 1980.

Rudestan, K. E. *Methods of Self-Change*. Monterey, Calif.: Brooks/Cole, 1980.

Sanford, N. "Social Psychology: Its Place in Personology." *American Psychologist*, 1982, *37*, 896-903.

Scarr, S., and McCartney, K. "How People Make Their Own Environments: A Theory of Genotype Environment Effects." *Child Development*, 1983, *54*, 424-435.

Schank, R. C., and Abelson, R. P. *Scripts, Plans, Goals, and Understanding*. Hillsdale, N.J.: Erlbaum, 1977.

Shepard, R. N. "Attention and the Metric Structure of the Stimulus Space." *Journal of Mathematical Psychology*, 1964, *1*, 54-87.

Shure, M. B., and Spivack, G. *Problem-Solving Techniques in Childrearing*. San Francisco: Jossey-Bass, 1978.

Simon, H. A. *The Sciences of the Artificial*. (2nd ed.) Cambridge, Mass.: M.I.T. Press, 1981.

Skinner, B. F. "Superstition in the Pigeon." *Journal of Experimental Psychology*, 1948, *38*, 168-172.

Smith, M. L., Glass, G. V., and Miller, T. I. *The Benefits of Psychotherapy*. Baltimore: Johns Hopkins University Press, 1980.

Snow, C. P. *The Two Cultures and the Scientific Revolution*. Cambridge, England: Cambridge University Press, 1959.

Snyder, C. R. R. "Individual Differences in Imagery and Thought." Unpublished doctoral dissertation, Department of Psychology, University of Oregon, 1972.

Spitz, R. A. "Hospitalism: An Inquiry into the Genesis of Psychiatric Conditions in Early Childhood." *Psychoanalytic Study of the Child*, 1945, *1*, 53-74, 113-117.

Stein, M. I. *Stimulating Creativity*. Vol. 1: *Individual Procedures*. New York: Academic Press, 1974.

Stein, M. I. *Stimulating Creativity*. Vol. 2: *Group Procedures*. New York: Academic Press, 1975.

Steiner, I. D. "Social Psychology." In E. Hearst (Ed.), *The First Century of Experimental Psychology*. Hillsdale, N.J.: Erlbaum, 1979.

Stokols, D. "Environmental Psychology." *Annual Review of Psychology*, 1978, *29*, 253-295.

Sundberg, N. D., Snowden, L. R., and Reynolds, W. M. "Toward Assessment of Personal Competence and Incompetence in Life Situations." *Annual Review of Psychology*, 1978, *29*, 179-221.

Sundberg, N. D., Taplin, J. R., and Tyler, L. E. *Introduction to Clinical Psychology*. Englewood Cliffs, N.J.: Prentice-Hall, 1983.

Sundberg, N. D., Tyler, L. E., and Taplin, J. R. *Clinical Psychology: Expanding Horizons*. Englewood Cliffs, N.J.: Prentice-Hall, 1973.

Tanner, J. M. "Variability of Growth and Maturity in Newborn Infants." In M. Lewis and L. A. Rosenbloom (Eds.), *The Effect of the Infant on the Caregiver*. New York: Wiley, 1974.

Taylor, S. E., and Crocker, J. "Schematic Bases of Social Information Processing." In E. T. Higgins, C. P. Herman, and M. P. Zanna (Eds.), *Social Cognition*. Hillsdale, N.J.: Erlbaum, 1981.

Thorndike, E. L. *Animal Intelligence*. New York: Macmillan, 1911.

Thorndike, E. L. *The Fundamentals of Learning.* New York: Teachers College Press, Columbia University, 1932.

Timberlake, W., and Grant, D. L. "Autoshaping in Rats to the Presentation of Another Rat Predicting Food." *Science,* 1975, *190,* 690-692.

Toffler, A. *Future Shock.* New York: Bantam Books, 1971.

Tolman, E. C. *Purposive Behavior in Animals and Men.* New York: Appleton-Century, 1932.

Torbert, W. R. "Empirical, Behavioral, Theoretical, and Attentional Skills Necessary for Collaborative Inquiry." In P. Reason and J. Rowan (Eds.), *Human Inquiry.* New York: Wiley, 1981.

Torrance, E. P. *Education and the Creative Potential.* Minneapolis: University of Minnesota Press, 1963.

Tough, A. *Intentional Changes.* Chicago: Follett, 1982.

Treisman, A. M. "Strategies and Models of Selective Attention." *Psychological Review,* 1969, *76,* 282-299.

Truax, C. B., and Carkhuff, R. R. *Toward Effective Counseling and Psychotherapy.* Chicago: Aldine, 1967.

Tulving, E. "Episodic and Semantic Memory." In E. Tulving and W. Donaldson (Eds.), *Organization of Memory.* New York: Academic Press, 1972.

Tyler, L. E. *The Psychology of Human Differences.* (3rd ed.) New York: Appleton-Century-Crofts, 1965.

Tyler, L. E. *Individuality: Human Possibilities and Personal Choice in the Psychological Development of Men and Women.* San Francisco: Jossey-Bass, 1978a.

Tyler, L. E. "Why Do We Have to Have Compulsory Education for Adolescents?" In J. C. Flanagan (Ed.), *Perspectives on Improving Education.* New York: Praeger, 1978b.

Watson, J. B. "Psychology as the Behaviorist Views It." *Psychological Review,* 1913, *20,* 158-177.

Weigel, R. H., Vernon, D. T. A., and Tognacci, L. N. "Specificity of the Attitude as a Determinant of the Attitude-Behavior Congruence." *Journal of Personality and Social Psychology,* 1974, *30,* 724-728.

Wickelgren, W. A. "Human Learning and Memory." *Annual Review of Psychology,* 1981, *32,* 21-52.

Witkin, H. A. "Perception of Body Position and of the Position of the Visual Field." *Psychological Monographs,* 1949, No. 302.

Witkin, H. A., and Goodenough, D. R. *Cognitive Styles: Essence and Origins.* New York: International Universities Press, 1981.

Yalom, I. D. *The Theory and Practice of Group Psychotherapy.* (2nd ed.) New York: Basic Books, 1975.

Young, J. Z. *Programs of the Brain.* New York: Oxford University Press, 1978.

Zener, K. "The Significance of Behavior Accompanying Salivary Secretion for Theories of the Conditioned Response." *American Journal of Psychology,* 1937, *50,* 384-403.

INDEX

❖ ❖ ❖ ❖ ❖ ❖ ❖ ❖ ❖ ❖ ❖ ❖

215